The British
Welfare State
A Critical History

John Brown

BLACKWELL
Oxford UK & Cambridge USA

First published 1995

Blackwell Publishers, the publishing imprint of
Basil Blackwell Ltd
108 Cowley Road
Oxford OX4 1JF

Basil Blackwell Inc.
238 Main Street
Cambridge, Massachusetts 02142
USA

British Library Cataloguing in Publication Data
A CIP catalogue record for this book is available from the British Library.

Library of Congress Cataloging-in-Publication Data has been applied for

ISBN 0–631–18044–3
     0–631–17192–4(pbk)

Typeset in 11 on 13 pt English Times
by Colset Private Ltd, Singapore
Printed and bound in Great Britain by
Hartnolls Ltd, Bodmin, Cornwall
This book is printed on acid-free paper.

Contents

Introduction

The history of the Welfare State in Britain has attracted the attention of many economists and political and social scientists as well as historians. However, this wide academic interest is only part of a far more general interest and concern. In politics and the media there are constant references to the Welfare State, and many people, who have no specialist knowledge, believe that they understand its character because they have lived through much of its development and its operation has touched their lives. In fact its history is less familiar, less immediately understandable and far more complex than even well-informed discussion outside academic circles usually allows. Perhaps it is just as well that the two spheres of discussion for better or worse have been largely self-contained, and that scholarly research has attracted little outside attention, for if there were hungry sheep looking up and asking to be fed, they might not find much sustenance in its general aridity and complexity. It would be cynical, however, to emphasize this point. The similarity between professional scholarship and public interest is that the same divergence of opinion is found in each. At one extreme the Welfare State is seen as an essential characteristic of a civilized and humane society, at the other as creating a culture of dependency, and more cautious or moderate views of different kinds lie somewhere in between. In these circumstances history can be enlightening, and it is therefore unfortunate that when it has lessons to teach, they usually seem to be ignored.

What was the Welfare State? What had it become in Britain by the end of the 1980s? These are the questions with which this book is essentially concerned. Neither is easily answered, not only because of the complexities of the evidence, but also because any attempt at an abstract definition of a Welfare State generates as many problems as it solves. It is nevertheless possible to define its meaning relatively easily in historical terms, and in Britain the key event undoubtedly was the Beveridge Report's publication in 1942. Answers can be found therefore through focusing initially on the crucial period of reconstruction planning during the Second World War and then on what led to it and followed from it. This is the approach which this book takes. Its great advantage is that it allows long-term continuities and discontinuities to be identified far more clearly than would be possible in a chronological account spanning the years between the new Liberalism at the start of the century and the new Conservatism of the 1980s.

A number of more specific questions, of course, need also to be asked about what has shaped modern social policy and administration and economic management. To what extent have these been formed by political agreement? What other influences and pressures have been exerted? How have conflicts of interest been reconciled? These or very similar questions have always been posed by historical debate. More recently, however, they acquired a new sharpness, as rightwing governments throughout the 1980s repudiated any effort to find common ground with their opponents and dismissed criticism of their actions as mistaken or motivated by selfinterest. This confrontational style of politics and the collapse of any dialogue between the government and the opposition, pressure groups and professional bodies naturally stimulated a reconsideration of political history. As a result some historians have argued that any previous agreement was frequently more apparent than real, and that divisions over policy between right and left often remained substantial. The main response, however, has been either to defend or to attack the value of consensus and to raise doubts not about its existence but its consequences. It can be seen as the product of informed debate and supplying the only sound basis for policy, or as a series of compromises which prevented the solution of social and economic problems. Welfare issues have always provided foundations upon which agreement can be built, and any examination of this particular area of government therefore carries considerable implications for this general debate. In the end, of course, political differences are not going to be resolved, and judgements about the value of the Welfare State will finally be personal ones.

1

The Welfare State: Definition and Interpretation

The Problem of Definition

'The Welfare State' is a term which for more than 50 years has been used in various contexts, including historical analysis, without any clear agreement as to its meaning. It is impossible to define precisely and equally impossible to do without it, even though its use has invariably involved implicit or unstated assumptions, which in the face of efforts to clarify them remain vague or can even seem incompatible. This lack of clarity tends to be acknowledged but discounted in writing on the British Welfare State. Perhaps this is excusable, since in the case of Britain the term is intimately associated with the Beveridge Report. The expectations aroused by that Report's publication and acceptance during the Second World War brought the term into currency, and it remained in common use, among other reasons, because of attempts to shore up and revise Beveridge's policies and principles as doubts gradually accumulated about their effectiveness. In Britain 'the Welfare State' and 'Beveridge' have been virtually synonymous. But this scarcely solves the problem of definition, since his aims and methods have been judged very differently.[1]

In 1942 Beveridge believed that his *Report on Social Insurance and Allied Services* would bring to completion developments in social policy that had started at the turn of the century; and he assumed that his recommendations, which promised finally to abolish want in Britain, would come into force in postwar conditions in which governments maintained full employment, a free health service and adequate family allowances. 'The Welfare State' essentially meant the operation of his 'Plan for Social Security' in this broader context; and in the event for more than a generation his implicit and explicit assumptions apparently had been justified. The postwar reforms in social and medical services seemed to work effectively, with poverty and inequality at least very significantly reduced, and in an economy managed along Keynesian lines unemployment proved to be even lower than expected.

What happened after the mid-1970s, as the long postwar boom in the international economy faltered, is more difficult to describe. The economic and social problems which emerged then cast doubt on what had been achieved, and also reinforced an existing uncertainty, which had previously been largely suppressed. Without any clear redefinition 'the Welfare State' ceased to be shorthand for a series of solutions to modern needs and sometimes came to be seen as a barrier to their solution. In a growing debate on national decline, which was a response to the British economy's disappointing performance, it had an ambiguous role as either an agent or a victim – sometimes identified as a cause of mounting economic and financial difficulties and at others as weakened by them. There were suggestions that 'the Welfare State' was in terminal decline, even that it described a phase of liberal collectivism, of which Keynes and Beveridge had been the main exponents, that was now over, but more usually changes of policy were interpreted as adaptation or restructuring rather than as breaking with the past.

Britain, of course, was not unique after 1945 in creating health and social services covering the entire population and in pursuing full employment. Along with Sweden this country tended to be cited as a model 'Welfare State' only in the sense of exemplifying the final stage of developments which were occurring in other advanced industrial societies. Gunnar Myrdal stressed in 1958 that social and economic planning was common to both the industrialized capitalist and communist blocs and required scales of taxation, public expenditure and bureaucracy well beyond the capacity of governments elsewhere. He also insisted, in a way that now seems both dated and perceptive, that rather than the ideological divide, the gap between highly developed economies and areas of economic underdevelopment, where adequate welfare services were an impossible aspiration, posed the main threat to future international stability.[2]

The commitment to planned services and economic growth, in countries where these seemed attainable aims, did not rule out disagreement over the best methods of realizing them. In Britain after 1945 the value of the controls over imports, prices, personal consumption and the allocation of materials, inherited from wartime, was controversial, and most of them had been abolished before Labour lost the 1951 election. Ten years later there were calls for new central-planning bodies as instruments of a more actively interventionist government, and within another ten years there were fresh claims that interference with markets and personal choice had been pushed too far. Until the end of the 1970s, however, such disputes and fluctuations of policy did not seriously disturb confidence in the effectiveness of planning and management, at least within the constraints imposed by military commitments at home and abroad and by movements in the international economy from which Britain could not be insulated. Balance of payments deficits and a sterling crisis forced the Labour government to abandon its National Plan in 1966 and to devalue the following year, but the only immediate result was that politicians of all parties placed even greater stress than before on economic growth as a precondition for improved services.

In Britain the trend towards increased taxation and public spending had started before the First World War. After the Second World War both were far higher than in 1938, but there was no indication that the rate of increase was likely to slacken. Rising living standards and expectations, sustained by economic growth, appeared to be pushing the curve of public expenditure quickly upwards, and in 1967 the first modern attempt to trace and explain its shape since the start of the century predicted over the next 20 years increases in spending especially on social services.[3] Much of this expenditure in fact was not on welfare, however this was defined – a major share was being taken by armaments and defence – but in both the long and short term social needs and demands for better health, social and other public services seemed the main underlying causes which were pressing it ever upwards.

By 1975, as measured officially in a way which was the subject of some dispute, public expenditure had reached 60 per cent of GDP. At this level it could be financed at least in the medium term by budget deficits and relatively heavy taxation, and whether it constituted an immediate problem depended largely on what view was taken of Britain's long-run economic performance. However, the temporary conjunction of a stagnant international economy, worsening balance of payments deficits and speculation against sterling forced the Labour government the following year to try to draw on the International Monetary Fund beyond the limits of its automatic borrowing rights. Its request provoked from the other side of the Atlantic demands for large spending cuts as a condition of the loan, which were unprecedented in the Fund's dealings with a major nation, and even though public sector borrowing was already being pruned back, there was considerable resistance among British ministers against accepting the terms. The lack of access to cabinet and departmental papers makes it impossible to be completely certain about the character of the negotiations, which in the end led to a compromise of cuts higher than the government would have made on its own but lower than the IMF's initial requirements. However, when officials of the Fund and of the US Treasury talked of British 'profligacy', they clearly had in mind spending on welfare; and equally in resisting their pressure, it was this area of expenditure, never precisely defined, that some Labour ministers wanted to safeguard.

The crisis can be seen either as a turning-point in postwar policy and a prelude to 'Thatcherism' or as a self-contained episode.[4] Public sector borrowing and monetary targets well below the final requirements were quickly achieved, and the loan had been repaid ahead of time before Labour lost the 1979 election. More to the point perhaps is that the upward curve of public spending was only briefly disrupted. The 1976 cuts were far larger, not only than any before, but also than any later achieved by Conservative governments despite their rhetoric about rolling back the frontiers of the State. Throughout the 1980s, though there were year-to-year fluctuations, spending was rising. How much was going on welfare depended on what items were assigned to this category, but its level suggested that it would be premature to write the Welfare State's obituary.[5] Its pattern perhaps supported a somewhat different conclusion.

For any real understanding it is necessary, of course, to go beyond generalities about the scale of taxation and expenditure and to look in detail at the evolution of policy. The trouble is that any attempt to do so at once runs into the difficulty of deciding what areas of policy come into consideration. Since perceptions of the constituents of social welfare have varied at different times, this is not a simple preliminary, and any definition divorced from specific historical circumstances inevitably raises some doubt or disagreement. According to Asa Briggs in an influential article in 1961, a Welfare State is one

> in which organised power is deliberately used (through politics and administration) in an effort to modify the play of market forces in at least three directions – first, by guaranteeing individuals and families a minimum income . . . second, by narrowing the extent of insecurity . . . third, by ensuring that all citizens without distinction of status and class are offered the best standards available in relation to an agreed range of social services.[6]

This definition is as good as any, but nevertheless it provokes immediate questions – what income and degree of security are to be regarded as reasonable, what services and standards are guaranteed, what is the nature of agreement, and how has it been reached?

If these questions seem more obvious now than 30 years ago, this is because prevailing assumptions have changed rather than because answers were ever easy. Then it was largely taken for granted that postwar reforms had led to a redistribution of income so extensive that class differences were becoming submerged in a common citizenship. The view that the Welfare State was redistributive, and that there was wide support for taxation for this purpose, in fact was commonplace for understandable reasons. The 1946 extension of national insurance to cover everyone in employment and its higher benefits had been accompanied by substantial increases in flat-rate insurance contributions. However, the cost of other major innovations such as national assistance, family allowances and the National Health Service had been met from general taxation. Moreover, the immediate origins of all these reforms lay in wartime reconstruction planning under a Coalition government, and Labour's displacement from power by the Conservatives in 1951 had not produced any major reversals of policy. Complaints that middle-class taxpayers on higher incomes were having to shoulder unfair burdens were so ineffective that they seemed indirect evidence of fiscal redistribution rather than significant disagreement over what constituted tolerable tax levels. Direct evidence that income differences were narrowing was apparently provided by Inland Revenue statistics, at least until 1962, when their dismissal as misleading by Richard Titmuss started a much more complex debate on the changing distribution of income and wealth.[7]

Nevertheless, even before this, doubts existed about the validity of assuming that substantial redistribution had occurred. In particular Titmuss had already written an essay on 'The Social Division of Welfare', with the subtitle, 'Some Reflections on the Search for Equity', of such originality, brilliance and, in some passages, vagueness that it was difficult to come to terms fully with its implications. In it he pointed out that the absence of any official definition of social expenditure or social service posed problems for analysing the redistributive effects of government policy. He also stressed that the move towards higher and more heavily pro-gressive taxation had been accompanied by tax rebates, such as the child allowances introduced in 1909 and the relief, changed at various times, on payments of life insurance or into private occupational pension schemes. All this was preliminary, however, to his identification of three broad categories of welfare – social, fiscal and occupational – which he saw as sharing the purpose of 'meeting certain dependent needs of the individual and the family,' and he argued that if these were considered together, twentieth-century Britain, far from moving smoothly towards greater equality, had also seen at times increases in inequality.

Though Titmuss was mainly interested in the light history might throw on current issues, his essay is the real starting point of modern historical debate. His conclusion that the search for equity had often been distorted or frustrated, raised the issue of what else had shaped policy, though he dealt with it himself only by vaguely asserting that 'the play of powerful economic and political forces' and 'the strength and tenacity of privilege' had often been evident.[8] His broad-ening of the concept of welfare also brought into prominence aspects of modern developments that had previously seemed peripheral. Old age pensions from 1908, national insurance from 1911, and the new public assistance, health and welfare services which resulted directly and indirectly from the recom-mendations of the 1905 Poor Law Commission, from the start had intermeshed with private medicine, charitable activity, tax provisions and legal obligations, covering the same contingen-cies of illness, unemployment, family disruption, retirement and death. As the lines between compulsory and voluntary and between public and private blurred, the principle had often been asserted that the responsibility and the capacity of individuals to support themselves and their dependants must be preserved. In 1942 Beveridge, for example, insisted that, 'the State in organising social security should not stifle incen-tive, opportunity, responsibility; in establishing a national minimum, it should leave room and encouragement for volun-tary action by each individual to provide more than the minimum for himself and his family.'[9] Titmuss changed the nature of this debate, for the next 30 years at least, by showing that the State, far from confining itself to the needs of poorer social groups, had patronized the development of a formidable range of fiscal and occupational benefits which were particularly advantageous to those on higher incomes. By the end of the 1950s it had become quite routine to compare the cost to local and central government of subsidising council rents with the loss of revenue from income tax relief on mortgage payments, or to point to how the spread of occupational pension schemes, encouraged by fiscal arrangements, was dividing the population into those covered by private superannuation as well as by national insurance and those with only the contributory state pension to depend on in old age. The extent of redistribution and the government's role in 'the real world of welfare'[10] more and more looked uncertain and hard to determine.

Since then the history of social and economic policy in Britain from the 1905 Liberal government's crucial innovations has been rewritten as a result of the progressive opening of cabinet and departmental papers to research, first under the 50 and then the 30-year rule, after the 1967 Public Records Act had reduced the period of closure. Lack of access handicaps the study of the last 30 years, when Beveridge's certainties that poverty could be eliminated and steady economic growth sustained were abandoned. Nevertheless, this period too has been subjected to substantial examination. Indeed the reappearance of heavy unemployment and other problems which had apparently been eliminated, along with political disagreement over levels of taxation and public spending, have given an added stimulus to rethinking longer term developments.

Increased knowledge does not, however, by itself define boundaries for the history of 'the health and welfare complex',[11] which remains difficult to map because perceptions of where its centre and outer limits lie have often differed considerably. This was true even before Titmuss widened the concept of 'welfare'. In 1937 Political and Economic Planning's *Report on the British Social Services* had no doubt, for example, that their core consisted of national insurance, public assistance (provided at the time both by the Unemployment Assistance Board and town and county councils), and local authority welfare services. Education and housing were seen as marginal, and the decision was taken, which in retrospect looks strange, to cover the first but not the second. In contrast the companion *Report on the British Health Services* emphasized the value of prevention as much as treatment and by including subjects such as water supply, refuse collection and food standards left itself open to the opposite charge of being indiscriminate. Five years later the Beveridge Report's survey of much the same ground contained nothing on education, virtually nothing directly on housing (which was subsumed under 'The Problem of Rent' in Part III),[12] and nothing on local welfare services, beyond a bare acknowledgement that they would continue to have some role.

International comparisons offer little direct help in deciding what services can legitimately be called welfare ones. At a modest level they describe different systems of pensions, health care and so on. At a much more ambitious level they can be used to build a theoretical model which purports to identify common or essential characteristics and to have some explanatory force. 'Macro-studies' of this kind, however, tend to have a passing relationship with historical evidence and to lead in different directions. One recent survey suggests that they divide into 'supply-based theories of welfare' and analyses of Welfare States as 'demand-driven', depending on whether factors such as national economic performance or the increasing proportion of the elderly in national populations are emphasized.[13] From the perspective of effect rather than cause Titmuss tentatively described three contrasting models, which seemed to him to be implicit in controversy or debate. In the first welfare is residual to private markets, its role to step in when these prove ineffective or break down; in the second it is an adjunct to industrial efficiency and achievement; and in the third it is redistributive, promoting social integration and equality. He believed that, 'The purpose of model-building is not to admire the architecture of the building, but to help us to see some order in all the disorder and confusion of facts, systems and choices concerning certain areas of our economic and social life.'[14] He consequently used theory eclectically, citing in different contexts the philosopher John Rawls on justice, for example, or the anthropologist Marcel Mauss on gifts in a way that left him open to the charge of lacking intellectual rigour. Since such references were almost entirely incidental, however, this criticism of the most influential and original writer on social welfare in Britain indicates more than anything else that an over-concern with theory can divert attention from matters of real substance.

In the case of Britain the Beveridge Report remains the best guide, even if it is not a perfect one, to the major lines of development. Its main omission was its silence not on education and housing but on the future of local welfare services, which had almost invariably been seen as central to modernization. A reform agenda had originally been set out by the 1909 Poor Law Majority, and in 1929 an essential preliminary had been achieved, when the separate Poor Laws of England and Scotland had been abolished and their duties and institutions transferred to the town and county councils, but the long delay had ensured a continued sense of the need for further change. In 1934 the councils had lost part of their new responsibilities to the Unemployment Assistance Board, which in 1940, renamed the Assistance Board, had been given the main role in dealing with wartime distress. In 1942 Beveridge recommended that it should eventually take over all responsibility for public assistance, with 'National' this time to be added to its title as a sign of final centralization. The constant problem both before and after 1929 was that different allowances and scales of financial support were inseparable from local administration, and Beveridge's concern was to secure uniformity. However, the councils were clearly going to retain responsibility for 'personal social services' (to use the 1967 Seebohm Committee's term), and despite his silence these were restructured after the Second World War by the 1948 Children's Act and by sections of the

National Assistance and National Health Service Acts. Over the next 20 years their importance within the new framework of policy was increasingly recognized, and this culminated in the far more ambitious changes of the 1968 Social Work (Scotland) Act and the 1970 Local Authority Social Services Act.

Nevertheless, whatever its omissions, the Beveridge Report possessed a unique and powerful coherence, and its impact on government and on public opinion could still be traced over 40 years later. Labour's 1978 Green Paper, *Social Assistance*, explained defensively why Beveridge's aims could no longer be sustained and indeed might never have been perfectly compatible. The 1985 Conservative White Paper, *The Reform of Social Security*, which broke with them more or less completely, still described the Report as 'by any measure a landmark',[15] and Conservative ministers sometimes explicitly claimed Beveridge's authority to endorse aspects of their policies. They could do so, of course, only through highly selective quotation. His name was invoked with much greater justification by opponents of the direction in which policy was moving from 1978 and even earlier, and in so far as these miscellaneous dissenters grouped together at all, it was under the vague banner of 'Back to Beveridge'.

Yet in 1942 Beveridge had claimed to be proposing 'a revolution' which was 'British' because it preserved a large measure of continuity with the past; and the ambiguity of this statement pervades historical debate. Though there can be no doubt that his Report was a landmark, it is one which has been seen very differently. The view that his 'Plan' failed to meet adequately the needs of postwar Britain quickly emerged after it had come into operation. Conversely the subsequent modification of its central tenet of universalism led to assertions that the Plan had a continued relevance in the late twentieth century.

The 1942 recommendations and assumptions, their origins and antecedents, and their implementation, modification or abandonment therefore deliminate the changing boundaries of 'the Welfare State' in Britain. At the core of social policy has been national insurance and its relationship, at higher income levels, to private insurance and, at lower ones, to the safety-net of means-tested income support, which has changed its name but kept its basic character, as poor relief or public assistance, as national assistance, as supplementary benefits or as income support. All 23 'principle changes' in Part II of the Report deal with these matters. However, the three assumptions in the final part, 'Social Security and Social Policy', were as important as the 'Plan for Social Security': 'Assumption A: Children's Allowances'; 'Assumption B: Comprehensive Health and Rehabilitation Services'; and 'Assumption C: Maintenance of Employment'. The first directly contributed to the Plan's essential aim of maintaining income, but the other two, in effect full employment and a free health service, had an independent importance. The grey areas on this map of welfare are housing and education. Conventionally public expenditure on both is assigned to the category of welfare spending, but Beveridge apparently regarded them as areas of personal choice where the maintenance of adequate income would ensure that the choices available to everyone were reasonable and fair. Local authority welfare services, however, cannot be seen as peripheral in the same way, since their history is inextricably linked to the developments which the Beveridge Report singles out.

Problems of Interpretation

To distinguish between problems of definition and of interpretation is essentially a matter of convenience. Titmuss broadened the concept of welfare to correct what he regarded as a stereotyped and distorted view of the Welfare State and its history. Briggs's definition reflected a similar dissatisfaction with existing accounts, which he described as vague and slanted, weakened in particular by an assumption that the development of modern social policy was to be interpreted in terms of gradual and inevitable progress. Both perhaps failed to allow sufficiently for the handicap of the 50-year rule on research, and a case might be made for a less dismissive judgement of a wide range of earlier writing. Nevertheless, their revisionism ushered in a much more complex historical debate, though no doubt with the increasing availability of government papers this would have come in any case.

In fact Briggs set out a research programme, implicitly at least, by identifying three 'considerations' with which an adequate history would have to come to terms, and listing five (or perhaps seven) 'factors' which required further investigation. He considered that the main phases of the Welfare State's development needed to be placed more firmly within both their economic context and the experience of industrialization and also to be dated with greater precision. The particular factors requiring research were the transformation of attitudes to poverty which had made the Poor Law impracticable; the way in which social investigation had directed attention to particular policies; the close association between unemployment and new welfare measures; the welfare practices which had been developed within market capitalism; and the influence of working-class pressure on the content and tone of social legislation. Almost as an afterthought changes in national income and in family structure were added to the list, with the suggestion that these might have been less important in Britain than in some other countries.

In surveying the present plethora of writing the initial problem is simply its sheer volume, and though bibliographical guides are available, by their nature their shelf-life is limited. Briggs's agenda for research perhaps has stood the test of time in the sense that almost all the subsequent stream of books and articles, encouraged by the progress of first the 50 and then the 30-year rule, could be fitted into one or other of its categories. But sometimes considerable paraphrase might be necessary to increase their elasticity (to accommodate, for example, feminist approaches to welfare under family structure). Research has also inevitably raised new issues without necessarily settling old ones.

Parts of the traditional account, of course, have been confirmed by access to official sources and other new evidence.

In particular, though important shifts of policy and opinion were occurring in late Victorian Britain, the conventional view that a decisive phase of change began with the Liberal party's return to power at the end of 1905 remains valid. Social and fiscal policy between 1906 and 1914 was the product of a new Liberalism, formed by ten years in opposition and three years of ineffective government before that. Its main components were the ideological commitment of a younger generation of politicians and intellectuals to administrative intervention, a greater understanding of the labour market and other aspects of the economy, the support of a more specialized and expert civil service, and the need to respond to the Labour party's emergence. As a result budgets between 1907 and 1909 brought in heavier and more progressive taxation (to finance higher naval spending as well as old age pensions and other social legislation), and there was a huge shift of priorities away from the traditional Liberal commitment to low public spending.

At the time the new fiscal and social policies were seen by ministers as crucial in their party's retention of power in the 1910 elections. Whether they were so necessary or such obvious political realism, however, has been queried. In particular two questions have been raised – did working-class voters actually want welfare legislation, and were the limits of middle-class tolerance being reached by 1914? There is evidence that outside the ranks of trade union and Labour party activists many ordinary people were apathetic or hostile to bureaucratic intervention in their lives, and that resentment was spreading against increases in income tax (which was paid almost entirely by middle and upper-class voters). It is uncertain how powerful these reactions were, however, since they failed to have any clear political repercussions. After the 1906 election the labour movement on the whole consistently supported Liberal policies, and Conservative opposition was hesitant. Whatever the underlying trends in the two general elections of 1910 and in later by-elections (which have been subjected to a great deal of sophisticated and rather inconclusive analysis), on the surface at least the government seemed to be gathering momentum rather than running out of steam. Lloyd George's 1914 budget, a few months before the outbreak of war, confidently aimed at financing further social spending by reorganizing and extending Exchequer rate-support grants as well as by further increases in taxation.[16]

A variety of interests had to be accommodated or reconciled as the legislation was brought into force. This was especially true of national health insurance, with its compulsory cover for a range of benefits of all manual workers (except self-employed ones) and all white-collar employees below a certain income level. Above all it moved administrative intervention outside the confines of deprivation, and its ambitious scope affected a number of important voluntary, professional and commercial groups and institutions. As a consequence the scheme has tended to be singled out as a case-study of the new politics, though the general conclusions to be drawn from either its immediate origins or its subsequent history have not exactly proved to be clear.

In 1908 non-contributory old age pensions had been introduced after a prolonged failure to find any contributory basis acceptable to the friendly societies and unlikely to damage their voluntary provisions against sickness and retirement. When a partnership between them and the State eventually was forged through devolving to the societies much of the administration of health insurance, the Prudential and the 'Combine' of other commercial insurance companies insisted on joining it; and they gained their objective through political lobbying, which has been described in fascinating detail by Bentley Gilbert in one of the first exercises in revisionism.[17] The medical profession had also to be squared. The British Medical Association's campaign against the 1911 Bill led to prolonged negotiations with the government, and even though the Act conceded some demands, others remained unsettled, so that until virtually the last moment it appeared uncertain whether health insurance could come into operation, at least in the form envisaged in the legislation. In contrast, for such a significant innovation the imposition of compulsory insurance contributions on employers and workers provoked surprisingly little reaction from either side.

In his foreword to Gilbert's book in 1966 Titmuss claimed that 'No-one . . . can with honesty continue to subscribe to the myth that lobby pressures . . . are relatively ineffectual in the party political system. . . . Nor, as students of the evolution of social policy, will they be able to continue to accept the placid, conventional, textbook account of the historical romance of "Welfare Statism".' His introductory 'Commentary' to the published memoirs of W. J. Braithwaite, the civil servant who drafted the scheme, had already made much the same point about the later history of health insurance under devolved administration, since once sectional interests had been accommodated, they had an inside role in shaping its future development.[18] However, the ideology of the new Liberalism stressed, as Michael Freeden among others has described, the need to harness the power of the State to a modernizing programme.[19] Health insurance was exactly the kind of ambitious experiment which justified this positive view of political action, and the government's concessions can be seen as evidence of flexibility rather than weakness.

Certainly the initial intentions were not substantially distorted. Liberal ministers had wanted to rescue the democratically-controlled friendly societies, which typified working-class self-help, from the financial difficulties which were resulting from a slowing-down of their growth and the rising average age of their membership. National health insurance was being grafted on to an extensive network of private thrift, which had been spreading since the mid-nineteenth century, and the last thing Liberals wanted to do was damage it. But in Edwardian Britain industrial insurance – the sale of small life or burial policies by agents of commercial companies who collected the premiums, weekly in most cases, from their clients and paid out dividends – was the buoyant part of the market; and the companies were naturally alarmed at the prospect of their customers as national insurance contributors being herded into organizations run by friendly society officials and exposed to propaganda about the better deal offered by non-profit-making policies. They therefore asked to be also allowed to administer the new State benefits. When Lloyd George gave way, Braithwaite saw his concession as a sell-out to powerful interests. In contrast Lloyd George always maintained that the companies' participation had been extremely valuable, especially in bringing indirect administration into operation, and that without their expertise there would have been far greater confusion and possibly even resistance among contributors. Certainly despite the concessions to their market rivals the friendly societies received, as intended, a fresh lease of life. Both groups were in an ideal position to sell additional policies to top up State benefits. The difference was that in 1911 industrial insurance had been highly profitable, while the actuarial liabilities of most friendly societies had been a source of considerable alarm.

Indirect administration ended in 1946, but the relationship between national and private insurance, if anything, became more complex with the rapid expansion of private occupational cover in postwar Britain. By the late 1950s both the Conservative government and the Labour opposition had accepted that an earnings-related element, with some graduation of contributions and benefits, should be introduced into state provisions to enable them to match private ones. This was a common agenda, the implementation of which began before the Conservatives lost office in 1964 and was carried on by Labour afterwards, but whether it represented basic or merely superficial agreement about the future was uncertain.

In a 1959 Fabian Tract, 'The Irresponsible Society', which caused a great stir in left-wing circles, Titmuss attacked the power in the hands of the directors, managers and professional advisors of the commercial companies from the huge funds under their control, describing them as arbiters of welfare, whose decisions harmed the rational use of resources. His immediate concern was to limit the inequalities which were being fostered by the private market. Apparently he also wanted to ensure somehow that private investment decisions conformed to the public interest, and his tract seemed sympathetic to the kind of socialist thinking that since

the First World War had occasionally made the nationalization of banks and insurance companies part of Labour's programme. At times he even seemed to be implying that the
companies exercised an effective veto on government decisions, though the rhetorical vagueness of some of his criticism
made it difficult to be completely sure quite what charges were
finally being levelled against them.

Certainly this is not an interpretation of the State's regu-
latory role in the changing and expanding private market that
can be sustained in any form either before or after 1946.[20]
Titmuss's attack apparently was prompted partly by the companies' opposition to earnings-related plans for national
insurance; and the 1959 Act allowed members of private
occupational schemes to be contracted out of the new
earnings-related State provisions. However, this concession
had been opposed by the Treasury because of the loss of
revenue it entailed. Boyd-Carpenter, the Minister of Pensions, had insisted on it as essential for the future expansion
of the private sector, but this was entirely his own opinion,
and all the companies had argued was that the earnings-
related provisions represented a poor deal for those on
average or better incomes. They had always regarded the
legislation as a political gimmick rather than a threat.

Titmuss in fact consistently used the example of health
insurance as proof that behind 'the Welfare State myth' lay
the reality of the 'Pressure Group State'.[21] The whole history
of the scheme, however, might as well be read as a case-
study of what Dahl and other American political scientists
have called interchangeably democratic pluralism or pluralist
democracy, which identifies pressure groups as intrinsic and
indeed crucial to the stable functioning of democratic politics.[22] Even so, as the exponents of pluralism themselves
have accepted, the involvement of vested interests in the
formation of policy, and the view that its aims are progressive
and rational, need to be reconciled, if only because the compromises necessary for agreement and stability may be
achieved at the price of stagnation.

More recently these issues have been raised in far wider

terms by the debate on corporatism – but again without reaching any very clear conclusions. The new social policies were developed during the transition from the late Victorian economy to a modern one of large firms, powerful trade unions, and an ideology of rationalization and efficiency rather than competition and profit, and they can be seen as one aspect of the State's response to the pressures and opportunities of this new industrial environment. Corporatism as a label for these changes (or near synonyms such as managerial capitalism) can be defined in various ways; and undoubtedly part of its attraction, despite its vagueness, is that it provides a general explanatory approach to what otherwise remain apparently miscellaneous developments. However, so much of the detailed evidence escapes even the loosest conceptual net or proves incapable of bearing any corporatist interpretation that more problems seem to be created than solved by its use. It takes a huge leap – though it has been attempted – to get from the increasing tendency during much of the twentieth century for ministers to consult leading employers and trade unionists on various issues to the conclusion that modern social and economic policy has rested on a tripartite agreement of the State, capital and labour.

The real era of corporatist politics, for which the lobbying surrounding the start of health insurance can appear to be a dress rehearsal, began at the end of the First World War. Until then local chambers of commerce and individual trade associations had given employers a not very effective collective voice. Representative national organizations only emerged at the end of the War, and shortly afterwards a concordat between the two main ones (which merged much later to create the CBI) left the Federation of British Industries to speak on finance, trade and the economy, and gave the National Confederation of Employers' Organisations responsibility for industrial relations and social policy. At the same time the huge expansion of trade union membership during the war meant that the TUC had become far more representative. In 1911 Lloyd George and other Liberal ministers had regarded its support for the introduction of national insurance as important, but over the next decade it grew much more powerful and influential within the world of labour.

These changes, as well as the 1918 Franchise Act, created a new political climate. The Industrial Conference of 1919, which brought employers and trade unionists together under government auspices in an attempt to reach agreement on postwar reconstruction and industrial peace, set an important precedent. Over the next 60 years meetings among ministers, civil servants, industrialists and trade unionists were frequent and normal. Ultimately such consultative proceedings, before being ignored or dismantled after 1979, had become systematic and formalized, as Labour and Conservative governments throughout the 1960s and 1970s struggled to find a prices and incomes policy to damp down inflation and contribute to steady economic growth. At times these meetings, whatever their character, can seem to be an aspect of lobbying, at others to occupy a middle ground between public debate and closed government, and it is difficult to determine in general how influential they were. The Thatcherite counter-revolution certainly broke with normal practice, but its refusal to conform can be regarded as symbolic as much as a matter of real substance.

'Corporatism is an extremely ambiguous concept,'[23] less because its meaning is unclear as because of the use to which it has sometimes been put. Middlemass in particular has seen economic and social policy since the First World War as largely an outcome of 'corporate bias' or 'the tendency of industrial, trade union and financial institutions to make reciprocal arrangements with each other while avoiding overt conflict'. He and Corelli Barnett have also linked this interpretation to Britain's long-term national decline by arguing that political stability was often achieved at the expense of avoiding real and painful solutions to major problems.[24] However, this seems a backward reading of history from the discontents of the 1970s. Between the wars agreement among ministers, trade unionists, industrialists and bankers was fragile or non-existent on many issues, and even the much more powerful consensus after 1945 under examination tends to reveal its limitations.

Whether welfare policy at any time can legitimately be called corporatist is doubtful. Perkin's *The Rise of Professional Society* is the most notable attempt to stress the government's autonomy at any time as a result of its possession of administrative expertise and its access to impartial advice; and without bothering to substitute the fig-leaf of professionalism for corporatism, political biographies and detailed studies of policy usually nakedly attribute decisions to the influence of individual ministers and civil servants or collective cabinet and departmental opinion. The problem with this approach is that professional groups often have (as in the case of doctors, lawyers and social workers during the reform of local welfare services in the 1960s) particular interests to further or defend, and that no clear criteria exist for judging a minister's or a department's performance. Neville Chamberlain's biographers claim, for example, that he was an extremely able Minister of Health, but his views on public assistance throughout the 1920s can seem as dogmatic and inadequate as his later ones on Nazi Germany are usually taken to have been.[25] In writing about the department where he made his reputation there is also a strange dichotomy – often harsh criticism of the Ministry's interwar actions and general admiration for its role in the creation of the National Health Service. The Cabinet's, the minister's or the civil service's independence in making the right or wrong decision is the only obvious point of agreement in this sort of historical debate.

Even the clear identification of the main stages of historical change has not become easier since Briggs more than 30 years ago considered that they needed to be dated more precisely. Access to government archives has reinforced a sense of how complex the interconnections have been between social and economic policy. Despite this, and despite too a running debate about their effects, the two World Wars still tend to be singled out conventionally as decisive breaks. The new problem, of course, is to characterize the most recent stage, and in particular to judge the claims that the period of Conservative government since 1979 brought about major changes. Both wars had an obvious displacement effect on taxation and public expenditure, which in both 1918 and 1945 were far above their prewar levels and never returned anywhere near them. This test, however, does not single out the last 15 years or so as distinctive, since tax and spending levels have stayed much the same as before. In any case the influence of war has always remained debatable for a number of reasons, apart from the obvious one that Sweden, the other model Welfare State, stayed neutral throughout both World Wars.

The conclusion that public attitudes and policies were decisively changed by the experience of the Second World War was advanced by Titmuss in his volume of the official War History (which appeared in 1950 despite inside attempts to suppress it because of its criticism of the civil service); and in a later essay he argued that war in general had a radicalizing impact.[26] However, despite its brilliance his official history now appears arbitrary in selecting three topics – evacuation, hospital provisions and the care of the homeless – and using these emergency measures as proof of a decisive development and growth of social services. On a more general level it would be difficult to compile an exhaustive list of all the factors which he and others have singled out to explain the impact of war. Among the most prominent, however, would be the State's need to mobilize and maintain popular support, the intensified pace of industrial and social change with military and civilian conscription and the creation of a war economy, and the heightened sense of national identity from the shared experience of sacrifice and deprivation. Nevertheless, the two World Wars differed in many respects, and the First was followed by a prolonged recession, the Second by a long international boom.

Recently a contrast has started to be drawn between the Welfare State's 'classic phase' during the 30 years or so after the Second World War and its subsequent decline (or reconstruction if a neutral term is required). Certainly the latest stage appears to have been shaped by a new Conservatism as much as the earliest was by a new Liberalism. The rejection of redistributive taxation, cuts in benefits and services, and growing poverty can all be cited as evidence of a major break not just with the postwar past but with trends since the start of the century. The notion of a classic phase, nevertheless, is ambiguous. There is a strange – not to say perverse – argument which turns the prehistory of the Welfare State into a lost age of humane social administration by pointing out that the Victorian Poor Law often provided the poorest members of local communities with a standard of living not too far below average.[27] The paradox depends entirely on misusing the concept of relative poverty, but its extremism at least draws attention very sharply to how ambiguous the notion of progress can be. During what is now starting to be called the classic phase of the Welfare State in Britain, social services and benefits in fact were frequently criticized as inadequate.[28]

It is no longer unconventional to suggest that changes in a particular area of policy cannot be written 'simply as progressive narrative'.[29] The use of 'simply' or any similar qualification in this kind of statement, however, simply avoids the problem. It is not solved either by various sociological theories which describe modern welfare as entirely functional to a late stage of industrialization, contributing to stability and expressing certain moral values and expectations. These may be useful in analysing the Welfare State as an international phenomenon but, however elaborated, scarcely come to any terms at all with the complex evolution of policy in any particular country. In a national perspective the competence of British governments, the intentions and effects of legislation, the resolution of conflicting interests, and successive shifts of policy and administration constitute in some sense a record of success and failure.

In exploring all these issues further, for the reasons already given, it is the Beveridge Report that again provides the best starting point.

Notes

1 The best discussion of the term's origin and of how it came into common use is in Peter Hennessy, *Never Again: Britain 1945–51* (1992). This is also the fullest study of the Beveridge Report in its social and political context.
2 Gunnar Myrdal, *Beyond the Welfare State* (1960).
3 Alan T. Peacock and Jack Wiseman, *The Growth of Public Expenditure in the United Kingdom* (1967).
4 Despite the lack of access to official documents the 1976 crisis has been written about extensively. Probably the best account is Kathleen Burk and Alec Cairncross, *Goodbye Great Britain: The 1976 IMF Crisis* (1992), and they see the crisis as a turning-point in postwar policy.
5 John Hills (ed.), *The State of Welfare: The Welfare State in Britain since 1974* (1990).
6 Asa Briggs, 'The Welfare State in Historical Perspective', *European Journal of Sociology*, II, 1961, reprinted in *The Collected Essays*, Vol. II (1985).
7 Richard M. Titmuss, *Income Distribution and Social Change* (1962).
8 Richard M. Titmuss, 'The Social Division of Welfare', *Essays on 'The Welfare State'* (1958), p. 54.
9 *Social Insurance and Allied Services, Report by Sir William Beveridge*, 1942 (Cmnd 6404), paragraph 9. This statement is quoted approvingly by the 1985 Conservative Green Paper, *The Reform of Social Security* (Cmnd 9517), and illustrates the danger of quoting out of context.
10 The phrase is used by Titmuss in *Essays on 'The Welfare State'*, p. 53.
11 Again this is Titmuss's phrase – the title of Part II of *Commitment to Welfare* (1968).
12 This section dealt with what Beveridge felt to be the major barriers in the way of his main aim of ensuring that flat-rate national insurance benefits would always cover adequately basic subsistence needs. Rent was a problem because of the wide regional variations in payments for similar rented accommodation.
13 Douglas Ashford, *The Emergence of the Welfare States* (1968).
14 R. M. Titmuss, *Social Policy* (1974), p. 30.
15 *The Reform of Social Security*, Vol. I, 1985 (Cmnd 9691), p. 4.

16 Bruce K. Murray, *The People's Budget, 1909–10* (1980). This is an essential account of fiscal policy, wider in scope than its title may suggest.

17 Bentley B. Gilbert, *The Evolution of National Insurance in Great Britain: The Origins of the Welfare State* (1966).

18 Gilbert, *The Evolution of National Insurance*, p. 8; Sir H. N. Bunbury (ed.), *Lloyd George's Ambulance Wagon, Being the Memoirs of William J. Braithwaite* (1957).

19 Michael Freeden, *The New Liberalism: An Ideology of Social Reform* (1978) is probably the best guide to a topic that has attracted considerable attention.

20 Leslie Hannah, *Inventing Retirement* (1986).

21 Richard M. Titmuss, *Essays on 'The Welfare State', second edition, with a new chapter on 'the Irresponsible Society'*, (1963), pp. 242, 219.

22 Robert A. Dahl, *Dilemmas of Pluralist Democracy* (1982); Robert A. Dahl and Charles E. Lindblom, *Politics, Economics and Welfare* (1976).

23 Harold Perkin, *The Rise of Professional Society* (1989), p. 286.

24 Keith Middlemass, *Power, Competition and the State*, Vol. I: *Britain in Search of Balance, 1940–61* (1986), p. 1. See also his *Politics in Industrial Society* (1983), and Corelli Barnett, *The Audit of War: The Illusion and Reality of Britain as a Great Nation* (1986).

25 Nora Bransom, *Poplarism, 1919–1925* (1979).

26 Richard M. Titmuss, *Problems of Social Policy* (1950); and 'War and Social Policy' in *Essays on 'The Welfare State'*.

27 This is the view of David Thompson in essays in L. Bonfield, R. Smith and K. Wrightson (eds), *The World We Have Gained*, and M. Pelling and R. M. Smith (eds), *Life, Death and the Elderly* (1991).

28 The term 'classic phase' is used by Anne Digby, *British Welfare Policy: Workhouse to Workfare* (1989) and Rodney Lowe, *The Welfare State in Britain since 1945* (1993).

29 Harry Hendrick, *Child Welfare, England 1872–1989* (1994), p. xi.

2

The Plan for Social Security

Beveridge's Recommendations and their Acceptance

Social Insurance and Allied Services, Report by Sir William Beveridge was presented to parliament at the end of November 1942. Within a month about 100,000 copies had been sold, and its initial sale quickly reached 635,000. This was an astonishingly high number for a command paper dealing at considerable length with complex issues, and measured in this simple way the public response is unique. By 1939 about 25,000 copies of the Pelican edition of the PEP Report on the British Health Services had been sold, which at the time had seemed an impressive figure, and which is high for any official or unofficial inquiry of this kind. Less than a thousand copies of the Fowler review's 1985 White Paper on social security were sold, for example, despite government claims that in terms of its significance it ranked with the Beveridge Report.

When the Committee on Social Insurance and Allied Services was set up in January 1941, the huge enthusiasm which greeted its recommendations almost two years later had not been foreseen and indeed could not have been predicted. The inquiry was an interdepartmental one, composed of civil servants apart from its chairman, into apparently specialist matters, and even the interest which had been aroused by the two PEP reports just before the war scarcely suggested that it was likely to have any great public impact. The last major official reports had been by Royal Commissions in 1926 and in 1931, on health and on unemployment insurance, and the immediate reason for the Committee's appointment was that the activities of another Royal Commission on workmen's compensation had been brought to a halt by the war.

As an expert on unemployment insurance and one of the great and good normally given such tasks, Sir William Beveridge seemed a natural choice as chairman. However, his appointment was less auspicious than appearances suggested, and in fact he was being sidelined from any immediate concern with wartime policy. In 1940 he had returned as a temporary civil servant to Whitehall, which he had left for academic life at the end of the First World War, and almost at once had made himself highly unpopular within the Ministry of Labour. He had a justified reputation for awkwardness and insensitivity, and his insistent lobbying for a more important post within the department had alienated the Permanent Secretary, Sir Thomas Phillips, who as a young man had worked under him, and the Minister, Ernest Bevin. Neither of them shared his own estimate that his experience and ability fitted him for the major role he wanted, and Bevin, who had come to dislike him thoroughly, seized upon the interdepartmental inquiry as a means of getting him out of the way. In the circumstances the offer of the chairmanship so badly hurt Beveridge's ambition and self-esteem that it was rumoured in Whitehall to have brought tears to his eyes. Certainly it looked more like an obscure end to his career than a great opportunity, which two years later would make him a household name.

Even on the eve of the Report's publication there was little to predict the public response to it. Beveridge had been keen to test consumer demand, but the investigation undertaken by G. D. H. Cole and the Nuffield Reconstruction Survey into popular attitudes to social welfare had managed to reach only impressionistic conclusions, the limitations of which had been exposed when Cole had appeared before the Committee as a witness. The only prior indication that the Report might have a powerful impact had come in January 1942, when it had been announced that the chairman alone, as the Committee's one independent member, would sign it, leaving his colleagues to confine themselves to lending him advice and help. This decision reflected the heavy weight of evidence which had been submitted in favour of a major reconstruction of national insurance, and apparently implied that far-reaching changes would be proposed, since the intention was clearly to avoid committing civil service departments to them in advance. But, even so, whatever recommendations emerged were bound to be extremely complicated and technical.

Although victory was no longer in doubt, there was still a desire to bolster civilian morale, and the Report's publication was stage-managed by the Ministry of Information. However, its existence quickly came to be ignored, and an Army Bureau of Current Affairs pamphlet on it was withdrawn, in conformity with a new official line that reconstruction issues were a distraction from the war effort. There is nothing in the surviving departmental archives to explain this change, and its significance is not completely clear. Reservations existed within government circles about the Report both before and after its publication, but there was no powerful or coherent hostility, though the switch from publicizing to ignoring it encouraged suspicions that there might be. In any case later neglect only showed all the more clearly how genuine popular enthusiasm was.

Nevertheless, despite its huge sale probably very few who bought the Report read it at all closely. Its six parts and seven appendices stretched to almost 300 pages, written in a mundane style, with occasional rhetorical flourishes, which quoted out of context, as they so often are, give a misleading impression. Some sections, especially the one towards the close on the 'Abolition of Want as a Practicable Post-War Aim', sustain a sober eloquence. More typical is paragraph 313, explaining the use of the terms 'exception', 'exemption' and 'excusal' in national insurance, which even a well-informed reader might have paused over, before moving on, as directed, to a fuller discussion elsewhere of the last two terms.

While the nature of the 'Plan for Social Security' in Part V can be relatively easily grasped, if only because it has already been described in Part I ('Introduction and Summary') and Part II ('The Principal Changes Proposed and their Reasons'), essential details cannot. The full explanation of the crucial concept of 'adequate subsistence' comes not in any of these sections but in Part III ('Three Special Problems'); and the 23 changes set out in Part II alter existing complex legal and administrative arrangements or create new ones. Listing them inevitably creates an impression of miscellaneousness: new marriage and funeral grants; higher sickness and unemployment benefit; changes in widows' and retirement pensions; universal insurance cover of the entire employed population; extensive administrative reorganization; and the assimilation of workmen's compensation into national insurance. Three appeared within square brackets to indicate that they were desirable but not essential to the Plan: the marriage grant; the retention of friendly societies as agents within national insurance after the abolition of indirect administration; and the nationalization of industrial insurance. Finally, not until Part VI ('Social Security and Social Policy') were the assumptions described in some detail about the context within which the Plan would operate. Early on it had been summarized as resting on three assumptions (children's allowances, a free health service and full employment), on three methods (social insurance, voluntary insurance and national assistance), and on six principles (flat-rate benefit, flat-rate contribution, adequacy of benefit, unified administration, comprehensiveness, and the classification of the population). But as a summary this was too brief and cryptic, and even many of those who bought the Report probably turned for guidance to the accounts of what Beveridge meant that appeared in newspapers and elsewhere.

Nevertheless, it is easy to understand the Plan's huge appeal. It promised substantially higher benefits both to those already covered by national insurance and to those who had previously been excluded. The existing health and unemployment schemes were to be assimilated; and a new uniform basic rate and new dependants' allowances (which had previously been paid only in the case of unemployment) were to be high enough to keep all claimants and their families out of poverty, even those without any savings or private insurance. The prospect of financial security in old age was also held out, after 20 years during which the contributory state pension would be progressively raised in real terms; and until then pensioners with no other income would be protected through an improved system of national assistance. Full employment, free health care, and children's or family allowances were also promised, not as extras, but as necessary for the new scheme's effectiveness. By reducing the volume of claims and consequently the required level of contributions, the first two would help to ensure its financial viability. Family allowances were to be financed from general taxation and to be paid weekly, irrespective of parental income, for each dependent child in a family except the first one. In general they would gear earnings more closely to need, and in the poorest households eliminate poverty due to low pay, while preserving the incentive to work, by keeping income higher when the head was in employment rather than claiming benefit.

The final promise was that the result of the Plan would be a Britain without poverty or want. Since this was embedded in the Report's daunting and wearisome complexity, it could not easily be dismissed as utopian, though no doubt many readers had skipped quite a few pages before reaching, if they ever did, the concluding sentences of paragraph 445:

> Want could have been abolished before the present war by a redistribution of income within the wage-earning classes, without touching the wealthier classes. This is not to suggest that redistribution of income should be confined to the wage-earning classes; still less is it said to suggest that men should be content with the avoidance of want, with subsistence incomes. It is said simply as the most convincing demonstration that abolition of want before the war was easily within the economic resources of the community; want was a needless scandal due to not taking the trouble to prevent it.

The new benefit scales were set out in detail in the Report, calculated at 1938 prices by a sub-committee of experts (A. L. Bowley, B. S. Rowntree, R. F. George and H. E. Magee), on the assumption that they would be updated to take account of inflation whenever they were introduced. They represented a belated application to policy of the poverty line, which had been used in social investigation (most notably by the first two members of the sub-committee) to monitor changes in living standards for over a generation; and all the experts had to do was reconcile minor differences in existing estimates of the cost of adequate diet, heating, clothing, household and personal sundries, for adult men and women, children and the elderly. Only the problem of how to treat rent, which the vast majority of households paid, and which varied widely throughout the country, troubled confidence in the validity of the calculations. And Beveridge solved it to his own satisfaction, if not everyone's, in the pages of the Report that came down in favour of adding a notional amount to national insurance benefit, somewhere between the high rents in London and low rents in Scotland and some other parts of Britain. He argued that what families paid to some extent was a matter of choice, and since better-off workers generally had higher rents, they would gain unfairly if actual rent became part of benefit. On balance he had no doubt that equity demanded the preservation of the flat-rate principle that everyone (in each insurance class) paid the same contributions for the same benefits. These were not arguments, however, that convinced even all the expert advisors.

In other sections of the Report Beveridge made the point that most people would want to live above the guaranteed minimum, and also that certain risks were not uniform or common enough to be covered by State provisions. Paragraph 375 summarized this aspect of his thinking by describing voluntary insurance as an 'essential' part of his Plan, at least in so far as it met 'real needs', and he insisted that the State must leave room for the exercise of personal choice. Nevertheless, he maintained that even claimants entirely dependent on national insurance would never be in poverty.

Though the Report was part of wider reconstruction planning by a Coalition government, the most positive political response to it came from Labour MPs. Even so, their party became so closely identified with it slightly fortuitously, as a result of the government's mishandled Commons debate in February 1943, when the decision was announced to refer Beveridge's recommendations to a civil service committee under Sir Thomas Phillips. Sir John Anderson and Sir Kingsley Wood, the main ministerial spokesmen, struck the wrong note because they were having to disguise personal reservations. Their unenthusiastic tone alienated many listeners and led to a Labour motion, condemning the government statements as inadequate, which, when pressed to a vote in the face of efforts by the party leaders to have it withdrawn, was supported by 97 Labour MPs, with a further 40 abstaining, and only 23, all but one of whom held office, opposing it. Bevin was particularly incensed, and at a subsequent meeting of the parliamentary party bitterly denounced its conduct, and refused to have anything further to do with it until almost the end of the war. The whole dispute, however, was emotional and confused. Though Bevin felt that improvements in national insurance were unimportant in comparison with the government's proposals on employment, which were eventually published in the 1944 White Paper, priorities in reconstruction planning were never an issue, and the complexity of Beveridge's recommendations made their reference to the Phillips committee an obvious and logical decision. Indeed it is difficult to see what the alternative might have been.

The main sticking point, at least to begin with, was cost, though Beveridge himself was not in the least defensive about the extra expenditure which his recommendations entailed. Part IV of the Report dealt with 'The Social Security Budget' at considerable length, and a long Appendix by the Government Actuary traversed the same ground. Table XII projected social security spending 20 years forward, from an estimated £697 million in 1945 to £858 million in 1965 (at constant prices), and if in retrospect some of the figures make surprising reading (such as the stable cost of health care or the declining cost of national assistance), at the time there was little need for critics to query them, since they left no doubt that his proposals would be expensive. The issue was whether Britain in the postwar world could afford the projected spending. Beveridge was certain that the cost could be borne, except in the case of old age pensions, and his attitude was summed up by the bald heading to the conclusion of Part IV, 'Social Security Worth Its Money Price'.

It seemed such good value partly because so much of the new spending would be financed by higher flat-rate insurance contributions; and Beveridge made the point that this aspect of his Plan also meant that it could be implemented without any political or social tension. He stressed the popularity of contributory principles and the extent to which his proposals involved horizontal transfers of income – from the young to the old, the healthy to the sick, and the employed to the unemployed – rather than a vertical social redistribution across class lines. Whether any levelling of income occurred in practice seemed to him an extraneous issue. His direct concern was to meet the objection that wage-earners on low pay could not afford the high flat-rate contributions which were the price of high benefits. He concluded that on the whole they could from the Ministry of Labour's survey in 1937–8 of working-class household budgets, and he also pointed to the savings on voluntary insurance, health bills and other items of personal spending which would become redundant under his Plan.

The contrary arguments were put privately in a Treasury memorandum written by Hubert Henderson in 1942. His views as a wartime economic advisor had moved away from his earlier radicalism, when he had collaborated with Keynes and Lloyd George in 1929 in framing a Liberal programme for economic recovery, and he summed up the disquiet which had been growing in some civil service circles as rumours of the likely nature of Beveridge's recommendations began to leak out. His memorandum argued that the cost was too great and would lead to high taxation which would hinder investment and postwar economic recovery. He also claimed that the principles of universalism and uniformity had been applied inconsistently, invoked when they suited Beveridge and ignored by him on other occasions. In particular he attacked the principle of a flat-rate benefit on the grounds that it took no account of local variations in living costs, and defended means-testing as a principle to be applied to tax-payers and the recipients of benefits alike. These arguments reflected doubts which were not always confined to conservative opinion or privately expressed. Bevin, for example, made clear his view that high benefits would be largely irrelevant in conditions of full employment in a speech to the Scottish TUC in Aberdeen in April 1944.

Within the government Keynes, even though he was an advisor on external policy, provided the main reassurance. He became involved in the internal debate when he was asked informally, along with Lionel Robbins, the head of the Economic Section of the Cabinet Office, and Sir George Epps, the Government Actuary, to try to prune the cost. In opposition to Henderson he argued that Beveridge's proposals were viable and realistic, not least because, as he pointed out, contributory insurance was a useful fiction, which limited calls for benefit increases and spread the financial burden away from income taxpayers. Other civil servants such as D. N. Chester, who had been the secretary to the Beveridge Committee, argued in a similar way that, at a time when pressure for improvements in national insurance was building up, any alternative to Beveridge's proposals would be more expensive. In general the advice which Ministers received was not at all alarmist. While the Report was being drafted, Treasury officials, and to some extent too Lionel Robbins, had been worried about its financial implications, but they had been reassured by Keynes's mediation and Beveridge's agreement to a transitional period for pension increases. Later the Economic Section was asked to look again at the postwar burdens which would be imposed on the economy, though in the end much of its advice was ignored. Amendments to the Plan in fact had the somewhat paradoxical effect, in the light of the limited disquiet which existed, of reducing the proportion of income from contributions and increasing its net budgetary cost.

Phillips and his colleagues, to whom Beveridge's recommendations had been referred, accepted in principle universal national insurance cover and the need for a health service. They had doubts about the government's ability to maintain full employment over the long term and about the desirability of family allowances, and their conservatism was also evident in their view that the Poor Law, however recast, would have to deal with an irreducible hopeless and feckless class. Their main negative conclusion was that the subsistence principle was impracticable. With some of these doubts muted or suppressed, their deliberations provided the substance of the White Paper on Social Insurance which was published in September 1944 (in two parts, *I, The Government's Scheme* and *II, Workmen's Compensation*). This undertook the intrinsically conservative task of dovetailing the Plan into existing legislation, sometimes through modifying it, and provided the blueprint for the 1946 National Insurance Act. All of Beveridge's bracketed recommendations disappeared. Also dropped was his recommendation in favour of an unlimited period of sickness and unemployment benefit (conditional only on claimants following medical advice or accepting retraining after a prolonged spell out of work), on the grounds that it was only prudent to retain some limit. The new qualifying conditions in this and other instances, however, were generous. For example, the self-employed (whom the White Paper described as a very mixed class, containing rich and poor alike) were brought into insurance on more lenient terms than Beveridge had envisaged.

The most striking instance of this generosity was the White Paper's endorsement of the decision, which had already been announced, to pay retirement pensions at a 'proper' rate from the start.[1] Beveridge had believed that the main threat to his Plan's financial stability lay in the demographic trend towards an ageing population and a worsening ratio between those in productive work and those not. He had proposed to tackle it partly by minor inducements to continue working after the retirement age. His main solution, however, had been to build up reserves of contributions, while only gradually raising pensions. The White Paper recognized that these transition arrangements were likely to prove so unpopular that they might quickly become politically unacceptable. The decision to abandon them, however, had been taken against the Economic Section's advice. It helped that national insurance, unlike private insurance, had never been fully funded, and that its compulsory character and the constant entry of young contributors meant benefits came from current income without the necessity of relying on accumulated reserves. The qualifying periods for the new pensions, only five years of contributions for those already covered by national insurance and ten for those who were not, nevertheless were generous. Older better-off contributors, who had previously been excluded by the income limit for non-manual work, received a particularly good deal.

Second thoughts perhaps came more easily because of the decision to abandon the principle of subsistence support. This had been announced during the debates in February 1943 when it had contributed to suspicions that the government lacked any real commitment to Beveridge's recommendations. The White Paper justified it by defining 'the right objective' as 'a benefit which provides a reasonable assurance against want, and at the same time takes account of the maximum contributions which the great body of contributors can properly be asked to bear'.[2]

The importance of this substitution of 'reasonable' for 'subsistence' was always open to debate. The concept of subsistence was always a dubious one, and within ten or 15 years belief in its validity had collapsed. At the time how its abandonment was seen depended largely on whether Beveridge's solution to the problem of rent seemed convincing. The Fabian Society, for example, continued to argue in its commentary on the Report and White Paper, just as it had in its evidence to the Beveridge Committee, that unless actual rents were paid as part of benefit, some claimants would be left in poverty, while others would receive excessive amounts. Such criticism, however, was scarcely logical in protesting, on the one hand, against a notional rent allowance and, on the other, lauding flat-rate principles as democratic and the only alternative to intolerable administrative complexity.[3]

The real issue was only raised in 1946 by the Labour government's decision not to tie benefits to the cost-of-living index but make them instead subject to periodic review. Index-linking during the parliamentary passage of the Insurance Bill was rejected for a number of reasons, not all of which were perfectly compatible: the cost would be too great; contributory principles would be eroded by weakening the connection between contributions and benefits; decreases caused by deflation would be intensely unpopular; automatic adjustments unless very frequent would still prevent the value of benefits from lagging behind prices; and real improvements might be hindered. James Griffiths, the Minister of Pensions and National Insurance, during the Bill's second reading also used the precedent of war pensions after the First World War as evidence that index-linking quickly broke down in practice. In fact, with real wages rising and savings providing a cushion, if governments wanted to be faithful to the spirit of Beveridge's thinking rather than the letter, probably it was only necessary to be clear about what 'reasonable' meant and to be prepared to maintain its real value.[4]

In any case the 1946 Act introduced substantial benefit increases and made other sweeping changes as part of a wider reconstruction programme. The 1944 White Paper on social insurance had accepted all three of Beveridge's assumptions and had set out the particular scheme of family allowances that had already been brought into force in 1945. The 1946 National Health Service Act for England and Wales, the 1947 Act for Scotland, and the 1948 National Assistance Act made other aspects of the Plan or its essential support a reality, and confidence that complete security and acceptable living standards had been achieved was boosted further by full employment. The 1944 White Paper on employment policy had pointed out that its aims were not a matter of legislation.

However, from the Economic Section James Meade had submitted a scheme to the Beveridge Committee, showing how variations in national insurance contributions might be used counter-cyclically to stabilize consumer credit and labour demand, and he and his colleagues had continued to work on this idea. As a result the 1946 Act allowed the government to vary contributions as part of general economic management. In the event these powers were never used. At the time, however, they contributed to the belief that despite the severity of the domestic and international problems facing Britain a coherent social and economic strategy was being pursued.

The Prewar Reform Agenda

The Beveridge Report had looked towards this future of postwar reconstruction. In doing so, however, it had taken up a prewar agenda of reform, and if the Report is to be fully understood, it has to be placed in a far broader perspective than wartime developments. In 1942 Beveridge's advocacy of sweeping change was balanced by his conviction that there had been steady progress since the start of the century. His opening survey of modern policy began with the 1897 Workman's Compensation Act. He then proceeded to list the 1908 Old Age Pensions Act, the 1909 Poor Law Commission Reports and the 1911 National Insurance Act as the bases for advances between the wars that had been made by the 1920 Unemployment Insurance Act, the 1925 Pensions Act, the 1929 Local Government Act and the 1934 Employment Act. He described all this legislation as having led, alongside the growth of voluntary insurance and medical services, to a recognition of social needs in Britain that was piecemeal and incomplete, but that was also already unmatched and scarcely rivalled in any other industrialized country. Despite his closing appeals for boldness to match the sacrifices that had made victory in the war certain, his belief that he was bringing to a conclusion a lengthy process of innovation and consolidation gave his Report at times a profoundly Whiggish air.

It is difficult to disentangle reconstruction planning completely from the prewar recognition of the need for major improvements in health and social welfare. In 1939 the government's apparent neglect of an agenda of reform, which had been drawn up in particular by the Royal Commission on health insurance and the PEP reports, did not appear to be posing any immediate problems. None of the items seemed particularly urgent. Indeed, while some had been added to the agenda quite recently, others had been on it virtually from the start of national insurance. As a whole the health scheme despite its defects and anomalies had always seemed to be solidly established, and since 1934 the unemployment one had apparently been rescued from its previous instability.

Nevertheless, substantial changes might well have come quite soon without the war. From 1937 inhibitions on public spending were weakening as the recession gave way to substantial economic growth, and though there had been no obvious response from central and local government to the PEP reports, within the civil service some of the reform agenda was being dusted down and looked at. In general the case for a systematic improvement in health and social services had at least been clearly stated and had attracted the interest of a wide range of 'middle opinion', to use Arthur Marwick's term, among individuals and groups from different parties and areas of expertise, who shared a commitment to central planning.[5]

Between the wars the problems of the unemployment scheme stemmed from its inability to cope with mass unemployment. In health insurance the three main needs were, first, to bring in the self-employed and white-collar workers above the income limit (whose plight had probably been worsened by the restriction of voluntary membership at the end of the First World War); second, to bring the wives and children of contributors within the scope of free medical care; and, third, to develop specialized treatment as a statutory right. There was also a need for higher sickness and disability benefit, which was partly obscured by the anomaly that equal contributions in any case were failing to secure the same rights for every contributor. Substantial numbers in fact already were covered for some free specialized care, purely because they were lucky enough to belong to an approved society with financial surpluses.

The 1942 Report also took up two general issues which had persistently troubled well-informed opinion – the need to co-ordinate national insurance as a whole and to establish a valid boundary between it and public assistance. Since 1911 the State had presided over two contrasting systems of income support (or three if old age pensions are added). National insurance benefits were paid automatically providing the qualifying conditions had been met, public assistance only after some assessment of personal means and household circumstances. A debate on their relationship started with 1909 Poor Law Commission Reports and the 1911 Act. At first, however, it was very confused, and not until the end of the First World War did it reach anything like coherence. In 1911 the framers of national insurance had wanted to keep it entirely separate from the Poor Law, which they regarded as contaminated by inappropriate concepts of deterrence and less eligibility; but this attitude was at odds with the Royal Commission's desire to construct effective means-tested services, which would not stigmatize their clients, and which would have a clear and legitimate role in meeting individual and family needs. Poverty in any case was so widespread that it was difficult to maintain that the two systems either in principle or practice were entirely separate. The whole issue was also clouded at first by the differences between the health and unemployment schemes, which initially were so huge that it was difficult to conceive of them as two sides of a single system.

Part I of the 1911 Act created compulsory health insurance for all manual workers, whatever their earnings, and for non-manual workers whose earnings fell below quite a high income limit. It provided three financial benefits – for sickness, disability and maternity – and medical benefit or free treatment by a general practitioner. Responsibility for paying the first three lay with the approved societies. Local insurance committees (on which the societies, town and county councils and the medical profession were represented) organized the last, overseeing in particular the panel of GPs who treated insurance patients in return for an annual capitation fee. This brief description, however, scarcely touches the scheme's complexity. For example, to qualify only the points made: there was voluntary as well as compulsory membership and exemptions from the latter on various grounds; until the end of the First World War a fifth ('sanatorium') benefit provided free treatment for tuberculosis; contributors were not legally obliged to join an approved society; and other methods of payment for panel practice were legally possible.

In contrast Part II of the 1911 Act, the unemployment scheme, was a cautious experiment, which had been designed in 1908 by Beveridge and his superior at the Board of Trade, Hubert Llewellyn Smith, to reinforce the introduction of labour exchanges. The intention was to ensure that the new exchanges were not swamped by casual labourers, and that some skilled men at least would have to sign on, when out of work, to claim benefit and to attract employers with job vacancies to fill. The two schemes were linked in a single Act only because it seemed better to impose contributions on employers and workers at one swoop to minimize possible evasion or protest. Virtually all they had in common was their tripartite contributory basis; and even though each was financed by contributions from the State, employers and workers, their financial structures in fact were very different. Part II had its complexities (such as subsidies to unemployment pay by trade unions). Anything like health insurance's blanket cover of the manual labour market, however, had intentionally been avoided, and at its start less than two million workers in seven scheduled trades were inside its compulsory provisions.

The successful operation of Part I, however, immediately made Part II's relatively narrow limits seem anomalous. The war distorted its expansion, when the attempt to extend unemployment insurance to munition workers broke down, but the 1920 Act finally made its cover virtually the same as health insurance's. The background to this legislation was labour militancy as well as reconstruction planning. Lloyd George's Coalition government seemed motivated, however, less by fear of political and social unrest than by a belief in a new era of industrial harmony; and when the postwar economic boom collapsed, it did not hesitate to risk unpopularity, though by this time militancy was ebbing. A belief in industrial cooperation lay behind the Act's permissive clauses, which allowed industries to opt out provided they set up private schemes with terms at least as good as the ones being brought into force; and dependants' allowances were introduced in 1921, in theory as a temporary measure, after meetings of employers and trade unionists at Gairloch (where the Prime Minister was on holiday). The real change came with the continuing depression and the Geddes Committee's proposals in 1922 for large cuts across the board in departmental spending. The Act's permissive clauses were quickly repealed, after only banking and insurance had taken advantage of them, since with the future so unsettled employers were reluctant to accept responsibility, and from the government's point of view there was a danger that the State might be left covering the areas of worst unemployment.

Nevertheless, the 1920 Act for the first time made it possible to regard national insurance as a single system, and the result was a vogue for 'all-in insurance' with its programme of administrative rationalization and expansion. Beveridge's contribution in 1924 was a pamphlet, *Insurance for All and Everything*, which his wife 30 years later called 'a foretaste of the Plan'.[6] However, after the 1925 Pensions Act had introduced contributory widows', orphans' and old age pensions, little was achieved beyond a list of further reforms. The programme's immediate appeal tended to wear thin once it moved from advocating savings through rationalization to proposing extra spending, and even apparently simple administrative practices proved to be surprisingly difficult to change. The integration of workmen's compensation and national insurance, for example, resisted sporadic scrutiny until eventually becoming part of Beveridge's remit in 1941. The abandon-

ment of the programme, or at least its indefinite postpone-
ment, was clearly signalled in 1926, when the Royal Commission on health insurance listed a number of major changes as
desirable only to rule out any possibility of implementing any
of them until a substantial economic recovery had occurred.

As well as cost, the two other barriers to co-ordination and
expansion were the indirect administration of the health
scheme, and the instability which plagued the unemployment
one, as numbers out of work persistently failed to conform to
actuarial expectations. Health insurance was not immune to
the depression. The 1926 Economy Act reduced the subsidy
from taxation just as higher contributions for widows',
orphans' and old age pensions were coming into force; but
it was actuarially complex, with hidden reserves which could
be utilized to meet various contingencies, including this one.
In contrast heavy unemployment immediately destroyed the
1920 Act's financial structure. However, if the aim was
co-ordination, the stability of one side of national insurance
was as much a problem as the instability of the other. The
health scheme – popular, uncontroversial, anomalous and
unsatisfactory – enjoyed a curious and limited success which
tended to rob proposals for change of any urgency.

Between the wars there was no real agreement about the
value of the scheme's indirect administration. Parts of it were
clearly little more than a sham. All approved societies were
supposed to be self-governing, but in 1912 rules had been
accepted that reflected the determination of boards of directors and commercial managers to keep power out of the hands
of their insurance agents by avoiding local meetings and any
delegate system. The Prudential approved society, for example, met annually in London, the quorum was tiny, and
there was no bar against the attendance and voting of com-
pany employees. Democracy, as Alexander Gray remarked,
amounted to a phalanx of typists. In 1926 the Majority on
the Royal Commission insisted quite rightly, however, that
friendly society self-government enabled thousands of ordinary people to experience public responsibility. They also
pointed out that contributors as a whole had no complaints

about indirect administration. The alternative view, given in some of the evidence to the Commission and accepted by the Minority, was that it only worked at all because of continuous central supervision, and that its existence was preventing the extension of national insurance as a whole.

What gradually sapped support was the inequity inseparable from this peculiar and flawed attempt at administrative democracy. The first valuation at the end of the First World War revealed, as expected, that because of different sickness rates among their memberships some approved societies were struggling to meet their statutory obligations, while others had funds well in excess of the necessary reserves. A schedule to the 1911 Act laid down what additional benefits a society might provide for its members to disperse excessive funds. (Profits could not be used, of course, either to pay dividends or to subsidize private policies.) However, though the situation had been foreseen, not enough thought had been given to it, since in 1911 the real fear had been that some societies would become bankrupt and be unable to meet fully their statutory obligations, and profitable ones had naturally not appeared to be much of a problem in comparison. By 1926, however, the Royal Commission was faced with arguments that the approved societies should be scrapped and administration centralized in the interests of fairness. The same issue was also raised indirectly by demands for the most popular additional benefits, free dental and opthalmic treatment, to become statutory ones. The Minority as a result recommended administrative centralization as the only real solution. The Majority, however, refused to do so. Their solution, a partial pooling and redistribution of surpluses uncovered at valuations, was opposed by the societies, rejected by the government, and in any case more or less admitted that under indirect administration all that was possible was to limit the growth of inequity.

Beveridge's proposal in 1942 to retain the friendly societies as agents within a standardized system was both a postscript to this debate and another awkward compromise, which also invited rejection, even if it had not been bracketed as inessential. In 1911 there had been a clear sense that administrative complexity was justified by social gains. By 1942 this was no longer the case, even though the friendly societies still had a huge membership, and the growth of private occupational insurance, which undermined them after the war, had scarcely started.

Until the war confidence that national insurance could play anything like the role envisaged for it by Beveridge in 1942 was also badly inhibited by the unemployment scheme's problems. The 1920 Act substituted a one-in-six for the 1911 one-in-five rule – which meant that claimants had to have paid six weekly contributions for every week on benefit – and the length of any single claim continued to be limited to a maximum number of weeks. As unemployment increased, these conditions had almost at once to be superseded in order to keep huge numbers of claimants from becoming disqualified. This relaxation was initially seen as a temporary expedient until an economic upswing materialized, and necessary too, in fairness to younger workers, who had not had the chance of building up a good contributory record before the recession started. Official thinking was further clarified by an inter-departmental committee under Sir John Anderson, which stressed that a contributory basis for relief had to be preserved in order not to throw the entire cost on to central and local government. In many districts, as it was, throughout the 1920s the Poor Law authorities found themselves supplementing inadequate insurance benefits or entirely supporting disqualified claimants and their families, with high local rates and borrowing as a result severely straining the local tax base. The Unemployment Insurance Fund was in deficit, and Exchequer support baled it out, but it was kept afloat too by its current income and its capacity to contract and service debt. For successive governments relaxing the contributory requirements was therefore as much a matter of self-interest as anything else.

At first a strict distinction was maintained between claims which met the old rules and the payment of 'uncovenanted' and then 'extended' benefit under new ones. At least this was the case until 1927, when the Conservative government accepted the Blanesburgh Committee's contention that in principle discrimination was wrong, and that all those who were genuinely unemployed should be treated in the same way. Even then the Committee's proposals for transitionary arrangements until common conditions could be brought into force perpetuated two classes of claimant. Throughout these years, of course, there was always a desire to return to something like the simplicity that had been lost. In particular the conclusion that it was important to look essentially at a claimant's recent employment record led to the payment of 30 contributions over the last two years becoming identified as a valid minimum requirement. But both before and after 1927 successive governments shied away from bringing this rule into force because its immediate effect would always have been to expel large numbers from insurance.[7]

In practice the administration and adjudication of claims after 1920 became an extremely complex mixture of statutory and discretionary procedures. Deacon has described the situation as one of 'conciliation and coercion', since laxer contributory requirements encouraged greater administrative strictness in an effort to limit their cost. Claims had always been disallowed if a contributor had become unemployed as a result of a trade dispute, leaving work without just cause or dismissal for misconduct. A new requirement that a claimant should be genuinely seeking work was introduced initially for uncovenanted benefit and then applied generally in 1924 by the first Labour government. It caused particular resentment and bitterness, when jobs were so difficult to find, and when labour exchange officials were under such heavy pressure from the Ministry of Labour to be vigilant. There was continuous official talk of the dangers of fraud despite the absence of real evidence that any existed, and in 1925 a huge jump in disqualifications, immune to any other satisfactory explanation, made it clear to detached observers that many administrative decisions must be purely arbitrary. According to the final judge of appeal in cases of statutory rights ('the Umpire'), whether a claimant was genuinely looking for work depended on his state of mind. His judgement also specified in detail the considerations which an interview or hearing might bring out to determine a person's mental state. But as the Morris Committee argued in 1929, unbiassed observers might legitimately disagree over something so subjective, and the second Labour government with some reluctance accepted its advice to abolish the requirement. By this time public faith in administrative fairness was in danger of being sapped.

Throughout the 1920s both Labour and Conservative governments shored up unemployment insurance in the absence of any obvious alternative. After the war demobilization and the re-adjustment to a peacetime economy had been covered by the 'Out-of-Work Donation', a temporary scheme of non-contributory relief, and the TUC slogan, 'Work or Maintenance', kept in mind how expensive this had been. Many on the right believed that large numbers of claimants were not genuinely unemployed and should be left to the Poor Law. They also wanted to keep public assistance low, believed that other deterrent practices could also contribute to lowering local rates, and were infuriated by what they regarded as the laxity of many Labour-controlled authorities. But the imminent return of 'normal' conditions was always expected. Even to define what these might be did not seem a major problem, and the Blanesburgh Committee, drawing on conventional wisdom, assumed that unemployment would soon be averaging 7 per cent. Like many other failed economic predictions at the time it seemed reasonable.

A reaction started with a hardening of opinion among industrialists and businessmen in favour of a return to actuarial strictness. The 1920 Act's collapse had been accompanied by changes in contribution and benefit rates, which disproportionately increased the employer's share, and the argument that this increase could be passed on to consumers as higher prices carried no weight with an NCEO leadership worried about comparative production costs and declining international competitiveness. By the time of the Blanesburgh Committee's appointment to review the scheme the Confederation's leaders wanted to return to the 1911 position with the employer's, employee's and State weekly contribution the same (or in the contemporary jargon 'equal thirds'). They disliked the relaxation of requirements, but on the Blanesburgh Committee Sir James Lithgow, who represented their views, compromised. In return for support for 'equal thirds' he accepted the '30-in-two' rule, and the Committee recommended unanimously that both should be brought into effect, though the second only after a delay to allow the effects of the prolonged miners' strike in 1926 to recede. The NCEO tactics badly miscarried, however, when Churchill as Chancellor and the rest of the Conservative cabinet insisted that the limits on public spending ruled out the acceptance of 'equal thirds'. The whole sequence of events lent an edge of bitterness to the Confederation's subsequent campaign for actuarial rectitude as unemployment, far from falling to around 7 per cent, increased dramatically in 1929, just as the Blanesburgh transitional arrangements were supposed to end.

After the 1929 election the darkening economic climate and fragmentation of the previous consensus, partly artificial though it may have been, left the minority Labour government without a coherent policy. Its collapse and the formation of a National government, dominated by the Conservatives, in 1931 led to another Economy Act, which brought the 30-in-two rule into force at last and limited the payment of benefit to a maximum of 26 weeks. Disqualified claimants became the responsibility of the Public Assistance Committees of Town and County Councils, which under the 1929 Local Government Acts had inherited the duties of the former Poor Law authorities, and then in 1934 of a new Unemployment Assistance Board. In theory at least the Board had substantial autonomy, and the 1934 Act was intended not only to complete the restoration of actuarial soundness but also to rescue unemployment relief from political controversy.

However, there was no real agreement that this final prewar boundary between two systems had any greater validity than previous ones. Ministers argued that the treatment of the long-term unemployed and their families had to be taken outside the vagaries of politics, and that the Board was a model of good social administration in combining uniformity and flexibility, especially in using a standard scale of income support but applying it with discretion. Critics held that in principle democratic control was preferable, and that autonomy was largely a fiction, with ministers behind the scenes exercising influence free from public scrutiny. The start of 1935 saw a wave of local protests and demonstrations, as about half of the claimants transferred from the Public Assistance Committees found that they were worse off, and during the next two years, until the scale and the regulations had been revised, claimants received either the old amount or the new one, whichever was higher. Afterwards the Board's history, on the surface at least, was free from tension. But this calm partly reflected the fact that the economic recovery was reducing its clients to a hard core of long-term unemployed and their families. Their circumstances, moreover, remained a source of concern. In 1937 *Men Without Work*, the Pilgrim Trust survey, found many of them living beneath the poverty line, some far beneath it.

On the other side of the boundary the new contributory requirements, coinciding with economic recovery, meant that after 1934 the Unemployment Insurance Fund's current income quickly began to exceed total benefit payments. These surpluses were highly embarrassing, both for the government and for the Statutory Advisory Committee, which had been set up in 1934 under Beveridge's chairmanship to provide impartial advice on the reconstructed scheme's administration. He and his colleagues found themselves faced with demands for benefit increases from child welfare groups and trade unions, which, if accepted, would have led to many claimants, who had previously been on low pay, receiving amounts near to their normal wages. They regarded this prospect with alarm, and their advice to use surplus income to reduce accumulated debt cloaked their real motive, which was to avoid increasing either the basic rate or dependants' allowances in order not to damage the incentive to work. This was how they saw the problem. There was, of course, no hard evidence that increases would have had the effects that they feared.

Wartime full employment and rising earnings transformed this situation. The Unemployment Assistance Board found a new function in 1940, as its old one disappeared, in dealing with the homelessness caused by bombing and other wartime distress, and as the Assistance Board its administration, particularly of the supplementary old age pensions which were introduced as a protection against inflation, justified faith in a fair and effective means-tested service much more than its prewar activity. Beveridge's proposal in 1942 to complete the process of centralization by transferring to it full responsibility for all public assistance was uncontroversial; and he also recommended that a new central department, the Ministry of Social Security, should become responsible for both national insurance and national assistance.

Nevertheless, on balance he emphasized rather than blurred the distinction between the two forms of income support. At times he apparently accepted that in order to deal with problem cases – those weak or bad characters who failed to conform to reasonable demands – national assistance would have to retain an element of deterrence. His principal concern, however, was to prevent popular consent to contributory principles from being undermined, and this led him to insist that, though both should be fully adequate, national insurance must be preferable. His ambivalence was encapsulated in paragraph 369 of the Report, which stated that national assistance 'must be felt to be something less desirable than insurance benefit; otherwise the insured persons get nothing for their contributions.'

However, despite minor elements of continuity, the 1942 recommendations are clearly not foreshadowed in the prewar debate. In the later 1930s the future apostle of high benefits, as Chairman of the Statutory Advisory Committee, was resisting pressure for modest benefit increases, and no one exemplifies better than Beveridge the shift in attitudes and expectations during the war from what has been called 'Baldwin's consensus' to 'Attlee's'.[8] While she was writing his life, Jose Harris discovered widely different and sometimes contradictory recollections of Beveridge among those who had known him, and despite her concentration on his public career her portrait was attacked by his stepson as unsympathetic. It is doubtful, however, if his character or personality was particularly baffling. As a whole the evidence confirms Lionel Robbins's brilliant sketch of him as an unhappy man, seldom at ease with himself or others, whose instincts, despite a streak of idealism, were conservative. Certainly there was nothing in his previous career to indicate his emergence during the war as the advocate of the case for high welfare spending. Harris identifies three stages to his life: his early years as an exponent of the new Liberalism; a sceptical middle age when his thinking had become largely *laissez-faire* as a result of his disillusioning struggles to implement labour dilution and food rationing during the First World War; and after 1939 a recovery of faith in the effectiveness of administrative intervention. Since he was always a conventional rather than an original thinker, whatever meaning is attached to these terms, his writings always expressed as much as formed the contemporary mood, never more so than during the final stage. The effects of the Second World War on attitudes to public expenditure were very different from those of the First. Treasury control in its modern form had been created by the civil service reorganization of 1919 and 1920 in response to the uncontrolled mushrooming of wartime spending. It was central to the economic caution of Baldwin's consensus and, if not destroyed, was seriously weakened after 1939, not only by Beveridge but also by the influence of Keynes and the Economic Section and other developments.

None of these points endorses Barnett's conclusion that from 'the Audit of War' the 1940 Coalition government emerges badly, failing to recognize the industrial problems which were exposed, and conceding instead to expectations of a better postwar society that were economically damaging. His case is maintained by its narrow focus and the single-mindedness with which it is pressed. *Years of Recovery*, after all, is the title of Cairncross's authoritative study of British economic policy between 1945 and 1951; and though Barnett

uses 'New Jerusalems' as a disparaging description of reconstruction, this is also the title of Elizabeth Durbin's study
of Labour party thinking on central planning from before
the war until afterwards. She explains in great detail why
improvements in social welfare and in industrial performance
were seen as complementary and not alternative goals; and the
conclusion that this theorizing, which was not by any means
confined to the political left, constituted a recipe for economic decline when carried into practice, is unwarrantedly
determinist and puts in a dubious context the immediate issues
which faced politicians and civil servants as the war drew to
a close. Cairncross has suggested that low British productivity
after 1945 may well have been a result of social redistribution
being pushed too far, but this is no more than an aside to
his account of Britain's recovery from imminent economic
collapse in 1945.[9] After Marshall aid had promoted Western
European reconstruction, most of Britain's main industrial
competitors in fact were spending around the same proportion of their national income on social welfare, however this
is defined, and no international league table singles out this
country as exceptional.

Arguments that public expenditure was too high started to
be heard soon after the end of the war, but for another 30
years or so remained highly contentious, politically and theoretically, and no more than a minority view. Political and
public opinion in general was moving towards the opposite
conclusion that more, not less, should be spent on health and
social welfare, if Beveridge's aim of eliminating poverty was
to be realized. One side-effect of this, however, was that on
the broad centre and left of politics almost as jaundiced a view
of the 1942 Report came to be held as on the right, and
it tended to be dismissed there not just as outdated but as
having always been out of touch with the postwar world.
Beveridge died in 1963, just after his 84th birthday and less
than a month before the publication of Labour's *New Frontiers for Social Security*; and Abel-Smith, whose advice lay
behind this policy statement, described the timing as 'for-
tuitous but appropriate. . . . The Beveridge system . . . is being

buried with its author'.[10] Later, just as second thoughts were
beginning to emerge in the circles where it had originated,
feminist writing reinforced this dismissive judgement, by
arguing that Beveridge had seen women essentially as dependants, failed to accord them real equality, and ignored their
needs as members of the workforce. Indeed the feminist criti-
que, in its range from moderation to extremism, and in its
balancing act between retrospective knowledge and a sense of
the historical context, offered a microcosm of the hostility of
progressive opinion.[11]

The whole of this criticism, of course, relies excessively on
hindsight. It is perfectly true, to continue with the feminist
example, that Beveridge saw women, in the words of paragraph 107 of the Report, as essentially wives and mothers,
along with their husbands members of 'a team', whose work
was 'vital but unpaid'. As a result his recommendations on
their position in national insurance – the payment of lower
contributions for lower benefits, their options if they continued working after marriage, and so on – largely perpetuated
existing arrangements. His marriage dowry proposal was
radical only in the sense that it had been rejected by parliament at the end of the First World War and before that considered and dropped in 1910. The 1931 census showed,
however, that seven out of eight married women were house-
wives without gainful employment. Beveridge in 1942 assumed
that the proportion working outside the home had probably
increased to one in seven by the outbreak of war, and in 1944
in *Full Employment and a Free Society* he projected a further
increase in their numbers in the postwar labour market.
Perhaps he should have thought harder about the implications of this trend. But it seems harsh to convict him of lack
of foresight when the case against him depends so heavily on
hindsight, and when he was sympathetic to contemporary
feminist causes such as the demand for family allowances.

The British health and social services can be regarded as
relatively successful and stable on the eve of the war, as ripe
for imminent reform, or as somewhere in between. But
Beveridge's assumptions in 1942 – full employment, a free

health service and family allowances, both of the last two universal in cover – would have been astonishing ones to make in 1939, and in comparison with his recommendations on national insurance the PEP ones only five years earlier seem timid. Nevertheless, there is a paradox – his ambitious Plan never worked in the way expected, and within a relatively short time its revision had become a serious political objective.

From the 1946 Act to the Fowler Review

Labour fought the 1951 general election largely on its domestic record in government, but by 1959, when the party suffered its third successive electoral defeat, much of this satisfaction with its past achievements had gone. Though general living standards were rising, the persistence of deprivation was widely accepted, and the postwar social legislation did not appear to be meeting needs either fully or in the way intended. National assistance, far from playing the dwindling role envisaged by Beveridge, had taken on a far wider one, and faith was weakening in the validity of his flat-rate principles and his concept of a guaranteed minimum. Doubts were growing about the basic adequacy of national assistance and national insurance benefits, and in particular, and despite the decision to pay the new State pensions at a 'proper' rate from the start, the living conditions of many pensioners were a source of concern.

For the next ten or 15 years in a sense the central issue was whether to shore up Beveridge's universalism or to move towards a greater reliance on selectivity. Proposals for change, however, virtually always involved some compromise between these two possibilities rather than any decisive shift in one direction or the other. Though the case was argued that Britain had become so affluent that State support remained essential only for the poorest families or groups, the Conservative party showed little inclination to do more than flirt with this right-wing radicalism, and the defence of universalism in principle that it prompted never ruled out the need for more effective selectivity. In practice under both Conservative and Labour governments major changes were made in national insurance, and national assistance was replaced by supplementary and other means-tested benefits. A parallel restructuring of local authority social and welfare services also occurred. In all three areas of policy the changes reflected a common acceptance that Beveridge's description of wants or needs had lost much of its relevance, and cumulatively they smudged so much of the line he had drawn between universalism and selectivity that they amounted to a huge revision and even perhaps the virtual abandonment of his Plan.

The subsistence definition of poverty, as refined by Seebohm Rowntree at the end of the nineteenth century, had been used with minor variations in a number of major local surveys over the next 30 years, and faith in it did not collapse with the failure between 1943 and 1946 to link children's allowances and insurance benefits to it. It was no more open to criticism than before, and in rejecting the calculations of Beveridge's subcommittee, first Coalition and later Labour Ministers were only cautiously preserving some freedom of manoeuvre in one area of public spending. In his third survey of York, *Poverty and the Welfare State*, published in 1951, Rowntree and his collaborator, G. R. Lavers, used one variation, the human needs standard, to analyse the effects of postwar social legislation, full employment and higher wages on living standards; and their findings suggested that the refusal to link benefits to subsistence had not had any serious consequences. Beveridge's promise of a society without want had still been realized. In York there virtually was no poverty – or to be precise only 1.66 per cent of the town's population was living below the level of human needs.

A re-examination of the surviving schedules, by Atkinson and others, has suggested that the degree of error was probably greater than the standard sampling deviation because of the extent of non-response from households, some departures from the survey's original design and a failure to check data. Also it is doubtful that York was typical or that one case-study provided a valid basis for generalizing about Britain as a whole. At the time, however, any criticism was muted or suppressed. Rowntree had first surveyed York in 1899, and again in 1936, and this third survey, published when he was 80, was taken as clear proof of the Welfare State's success.

Nevertheless, when Peter Townsend a few years later described the struggle of many old age pensioners in Bethnal Green to live on an inadequate income, subsistence definitions of human needs seemed to him to be so evidently invalid, in ignoring normal expectations and priorities in personal spending, that he found it difficult to understand how they could ever have been influential. In fact they had always been open to criticism, even on the one point conceded by him, that minimum nutritional needs could possibly be measured scientifically. Extremely few people, certainly not those living in poverty, had such an accurate knowledge of vitamin and calorific values that they could make the best use of the low sums of money allowed for the purchase of food by subsistence definitions, and in the 1930s John Boyd Orr had been the most notable scientist to insist that an adequate diet could only be defined in optimal terms. Criticism had been blunted by the subsistence poverty line's other function, to monitor progress, and once it became redundant for this purpose, as it did with the third York survey, its protective utility disappeared. The conclusion that virtually no poverty remained in Britain was contradicted by growing evidence of substantial material deprivation not only among the elderly, who were the first to attract concern, but also other groups. The analysis of class inequalities was encouraged by the Registrar General's division of the population into five classes for the first time in the 1951 census, which highlighted variations in life expectancy according to social class; and the coincidence of poorer health, lower income and other indicators of social disadvantage in inner cities and peripheral municipal estates showed too that class segregation had remained largely unaffected by postwar housing policies.

The new definitions of relative poverty, which became

current, also reflected the great outburst of consumer spending which began as rationing finally ended. Higher consumption altered perceptions of acceptable living standards and led to a widespread feeling that the gap between the poorest and the rest of society should not be allowed to become too great. As a result in 1959 the Conservative government raised national assistance more than was necessary to compensate for inflation since the last increase on the grounds that the poorest deserved a share in national prosperity. Complaints were voiced that taxation was too high and too redistributive, but economic growth could always square the circle between promises of no further increases and of better services, and Gaitskell during the 1959 election promised both if Labour won. However, the balance of public debate was shifting, the co-existence of affluence and squalor had become a cliché of political rhetoric, and the only uncertainty was the extent to which poverty and inequality could be equated.

This last point was addressed by new definitions of relative poverty without full agreement ever being reached. The most straightforward procedure was to take the number of households on national assistance before 1966 or supplementary benefit afterwards as measuring poverty. It was necessary, however, to allow for the failure to apply among those who were eligible, and also to take into account those on the margin of eligibility. In 1965 Abel-Smith and Townsend used as a poverty line the basic national assistance rate plus 40 per cent. By the early 1970s the official publication, *Social Trends*, was estimating both the numbers of families eligible for supplementary benefit and with incomes 10 and 20 per cent higher. Some addition seemed justifiable because administrative practices (which had been inherited from the Poor Law and the Unemployment Assistance Board) meant that in assessing the means of applicants for national assistance, and later for supplementary benefit, some personal income was disregarded and extra discretionary payments were often made.

Nevertheless, different procedures could lead to huge

variations in findings. The number of households in Britain in poverty during 1974-6, for example, was 912,000, if eligibility for supplementary benefit was used, but rose to 2,360,000, if households with an income 10 per cent above the basic rate were added, and an adjustment made for inflation. There was too the obvious paradox that increases in the basic rate, whether real improvements or not, at once produced higher estimates of poverty. Inflation and the absence of any systematic linking of benefits to prices, except for a brief period in the later 1970s, also contributed to the uncertainty over whether real or formal changes were being measured. In fact monitoring became extremely difficult, as was demonstrated very clearly in 1970, when, just before it lost the election, the Labour government faced accusations that it had presided over increasing poverty. The dispute between it and its critics, who were mainly its natural supporters, was virtually unresolvable, because a number of possible comparisons, taking account of changes at different times in taxation as well as various benefit rates, led to different conclusions.

An alternative method of calculation involved taking households which had income less than half of average earnings as living in poverty (or some procedure like this, using average manual wages or some similar slight variation). It was particularly useful for making international comparisons but equally open to criticism that it was a formal measurement rather than one of real need. Townsend tried to escape from these difficulties and to develop a consistent and objective standard, but his ambitious attempt failed because the index of deprivation, which he constructed, was too elaborate to be easily used, and some of the items on it were open to objection.[12]

The main source of concern remained consistently the numbers of individuals or households receiving means-tested support, and any increase was regarded as dismaying. At the start of national assistance over 1,750,000 people by late 1949 were receiving weekly allowances or single payments, about one in 30 of the total population, which was a higher proportion than on outdoor poor relief at the beginning of the century. By 1965, just before its replacement by supplementary benefit, the number had risen to about 2,847,000 or one in 18. Just as disturbing was the knowledge that many more people were eligible and failing to apply. Immediately before its abolition, for example, about a million old age pensioners entitled to it were calculated not to be receiving national assistance.

Since mainly the elderly were failing to apply, it was assumed, perhaps too readily, that an inheritance of fear and dislike from the Poor Law had always stigmatized the Board's work. Certainly by the end of the 1950s national assistance had come to be widely regarded as a residual service with a Poor Law past, intrusive and associated with personal failure, and it had become commonplace to think that its whole character tended to demoralize applicants and to deter potential ones. Only later did the failure to take up newly created means-tested services such as family income support, which was introduced in 1971, suggest that the underlying causes might be more diverse and in many cases possibly due simply to lack of information or regulations which were difficult to understand. Take up was also found to be particularly low when only small sums of money were involved. But although all means-tested services suffered from the same problem, degrees of immunity were evident in puzzling differences in take-up rates. The complex sources of stigmatization in administrative practices and individual and community attitudes were perceptively examined by Olive Stevenson at the government's request.[13] Long before this, however, Labour's claim in its 1951 election manifesto to have created in national assistance a form of means-tested income support that was free from deterrence had been destroyed, and in 1962 *New Frontiers for Social Security* promised to replace it by other arrangements which would be entirely free from its faults.

This aspect of the party's policy before its narrow victory in the 1964 election, however, was only the minor part of a broader strategy. Selectivity was still to be the maidservant of universalism, and *New Frontiers* placed the main emphasis on reforming national insurance. Richard Crossman, the politician mainly active in developing Labour's programme, and his advisors had no doubt that they wanted to retain Beveridge's division of responsibility. However, if national insurance was to continue to play the dominant role, they believed that his commitment to high benefits needed to be reinforced, and its character as regressive taxation more openly acknowledged and moderated. It needed to be placed, in Abel-Smith's words, on 'a wage-related basis', and when he described *New Frontiers* as burying the Beveridge system, he meant essentially the abandonment of flat-rate principles.

The grave had been ready since 1959, when the Conservative government had graduated national insurance contributions in an attempt to curb the rising cost of social security, especially of retirement pensions, which were consuming two-thirds of the total bill. A few years earlier the Phillips Committee had argued that the financial burden was bound to grow even heavier as the population aged, and that the only solution was to shift more of it on to contributors. The 1959 Act as a result moved in this direction, though without any real decision. Graduated payments were introduced, only a small proportion of which would eventually return to those paying them as enhancements to their pension, but they were such modest additions to the flat weekly rate in the case of higher incomes that the poll-tax character of national insurance was scarcely modified at all. Titmuss had severely criticized the Phillips Committee for revising downwards previous projections of the population of pensionable age but discounting this and other evidence, such as the growing numbers of women in employment, that allowed a more optimistic assessment than its own of the future. At best the Act in the light of his criticism could be regarded as a missed opportunity, which opened up new possibilities without exploiting them adequately, and at worst as making national insurance even more regressive by shifting a greater share of the total cost on to contributors.

New Frontiers set out two objectives: to relate contributions more closely to the ability to pay, and to ensure that State pensions came nearer to maintaining in retirement the previous living standards of contributors. Extra payments would lead ultimately to higher pensions, but those on low pay would benefit from a substantial levelling-up, since only about half their wage-related contributions would return to individual contributors, leaving the rest available for improving the basic rate. Graduation would also be extended to other insurance benefits, so that normal living standards would be better protected during unemployment and illness as well as in old age, but this was a subsidiary matter. The main problem was that a State pension too low to meet personal retirement needs adequately was still consuming a huge share of total welfare spending. Labour was confident in the run up to the 1964 election that it had the solution. Moreover, if national insurance ultimately provided better pensions, much of the pressure would be taken off national assistance or whatever replaced it, even if this could not happen immediately and some interim arrangements remained necessary.

Flat-rate principles had been killed partly by the redefinition of poverty and partly by the size of the social security bill. The third murderer was the postwar growth of private occupational insurance. From a modest base, created between the wars mainly by the Legal and General's sale of group policies to small and medium-sized firms, its huge expansion after 1945 rapidly changed the private market as significantly as the friendly societies and industrial insurance had during the later nineteenth century. Occupational schemes at first covered mainly white-collar employment but then widening areas of manual work as well, and though their quality varied, the position of those left outside was unenviable. There was very little belief, however, that national insurance as a result was becoming less relevant. Labour's aim was to make the State sector as attractive as the private one even for those covered by occupational schemes. During the 1964 election the party's slogan, retirement on half-pay for all, no doubt represented a considerable simplification, since new provisions for State pensions, whatever their character, would take a long time to mature fully, but it also undoubtedly held out an attractive goal.

Despite Labour's victory the new frontiers were not reached until ten years later. The 1966 National Insurance Act extended graduation to unemployment and sickness benefits without allowing any contracting out, which was starting with the minor rather than major inequality, since at the time about 16 million were covered for occupational sick pay, compared with the nine million in private superannuation schemes. A Pensions Bill was before parliament in 1970, but was sacrificed to the timing of the June election, which Labour unexpectedly lost. A Conservative Social Security Act at least reached the statute book in 1973, but it proved to be still-born, when Labour returned to power the following year. State Earnings Related Pensions (or SERPS) were finally introduced in 1975, in circumstances very different from those of more than a decade earlier, when the commitment to them had been made.

Shortly before his death Titmuss described the fundamentally different objectives of Labour's lost Bill of 1970 and the abortive Conservative Act of 1973. The first aimed to create State pensions which would have matched those of the private sector. Actuarial concerns had been set aside in the interests of equity, and particular generosity was to have been shown to those on low pay or with a broken pattern of employment, such as the great majority of women. The second would have institutionalized the inferiority of State pensions. Actuarial considerations were dominant, and not only was it non-redistributive but some of its provisions actually favoured the better-off. Its provisions seemed to him to be singularly out of touch with the more fluid society which was emerging in Britain, and which was characterized by changing patterns of education and training, more part-time work and greater occupational mobility.[14] Nevertheless, these different approaches by the two parties perhaps surprisingly in the end converged, and the 1975 Act was uncontroversial. It has been called not so much the best scheme for the early twenty-first century as the one on which at the time all parties and interests could agree, and the second point certainly is true.[15] Its provisions, framed after wide consultations, allowed contracting-out for those covered by private occupational schemes, and it ended up as an agreed measure which the Conservative opposition accepted. Pension plans, whatever their character, were being made for the next generation, with Labour's taking 20 years to mature and the Conservatives' 40, and the Bill was protected by its lack of immediacy, its complexity and a general desire to end uncertainty as well as by the process of consultation.

Virtually the last expression of consensus and the last occasion on which national insurance was confidently assigned a central role, the Act stood at the end of a road which went back to 1946. Titmuss's more fluid society was stagnating into one of heavy unemployment and high inflation, and the growing incidence of family break-down was only perhaps the most obvious sign that actual needs were becoming distanced more than before from the common risks which Beveridge had recognized in 1942. But it was a fault in the 1944 White Paper rather than in the Plan that was exposed by the new conditions. As long as unemployment remained low, and much of it frictional, the rejection of Beveridge's recommendation that benefit should run as long as need lasted – possibly subject to some retraining requirement – scarcely mattered. However, with full employment collapsing the limitation of any claim to a maximum number of weeks, along with the contributory requirements for requalification, meant that many of the unemployed, just as in the 1920s, found themselves not only out of work but also outside national insurance.

Even for the advocates of greater selectivity this represented at best a Pyrrhic victory. Great strains were being placed on the supplementary benefits system at a time when the introduction of other means-tested provisions between 1971 and 1973 was also threatening its coherence. A huge shift of dependency was occurring, but as it was largely unintentional and had unforeseen consequences, a dispassionate commitment to selectivity, as opposed to an ideological one, was difficult to sustain. Major anomalies had been created by the new provisions not only through their interaction with supplementary benefits but also with tax thresholds and low wages. A sense that policy was out of control, and that options were narrowing, was evident in the Labour government's review of supplementary benefits in 1978. It was initiated on the basis that any proposals it eventually made must not involve extra spending, and as a result it could do little more than emphasize that a gap between intentions and effects had widened so much that the scheme was being forced to play a role for which it had been 'neither designed nor subsequently adapted'.[16]

All this was a far cry from 1964, when Labour won the election confident that it could provide effective means-tested support within the framework of universalism. Two different promises had been made then: first, that the abolition of the National Assistance Board, when it came, would amount to more than a change of name; and, second, that in the interim old age pensioners would be guaranteed other financial support, if they needed it, entirely separate from national assistance. Labour's aim was to move towards some impersonal and comprehensive process of assessment which would avoid stigmatization and ensure full take-up, and various statements and speeches before the election suggested that income tax returns could be used for this purpose. Indeed for a time it even looked as if the National Assistance Board's successor might be the Inland Revenue. The idea had an attractive simplicity – while most people would continue to receive on the basis of their annual return a statement of their tax liability under PAYE, a minority could be negatively assessed and receive instead a notice of the credits due to them, which they could draw through the Post Office, to raise their income to a guaranteed minimum.

Shortly after the Labour government's formation there was an embarrassed announcement that this promise of a guaranteed income through negative assessment could not be honoured. The Inland Revenue apparently could not cope with the extra administrative burdens. In any case, the realization had dawned that annual returns would be an extremely inflexible way of dealing with changing personal circumstances, certainly in comparison with national assistance, which allowed decisions to be quickly revised, and which often made discretionary payments. Whether these unforeseen difficulties were insuperable is perhaps not finally clear. After all, national health insurance, which had often been condemned beforehand as an administrative nightmare, turned out to work in practice; and the idea of negative tax assessments occasionally resurfaced later, both in proposals of a vague 'Back to Beveridge' kind and in some right-wing thinking.

The 1966 Social Security Act provided an escape from the débâcle. Another promise, however, could be said to have been broken, since little more than names were changed. The Supplementary Benefits Commission took over from the National Assistance Board, and the entitlement to supplementary benefit replaced the right to national assistance (providing the opportunity for a debate on why 'entitlements' might be more desirable than 'rights'). The Commission was briefly part of a new Ministry of Social Security, which almost at once disappeared in a further reorganization of central government into the Department of Health and Social Security. At a local level, though regulations were simplified, assessments continued to be made by the same officials, essentially under the same procedures, with certain income disregarded and discretionary payments allowed. The Act was hailed as a success because claims for supplementary benefit at the start were considerably higher than for national assistance immediately before its abolition. But Atkinson's examination of the statistics in 1970 showed that this reflected the publicity accompanying the legislation and the more generous scale of the payments and disregards, and that among those eligible there was still a significant reluctance to apply.

By the time of Labour's review in 1978 take-up wavered between 70 and 75 per cent. The Commission's clientage had also changed. The unemployed and single parents had become far more numerous and, if dependants were counted, for the first time old age pensioners were in a minority. The extent to which stigma had waned or not was difficult to judge.

Welfare rights organizations had become active in encouraging claims, but Field's contention that this poverty lobby had transformed public attitudes seems dubious.[17] Claimants themselves proved to be diverse in their reactions and often confused, when asked whether benefits were adequate, open to abuse or a right rather than a charity. The most obvious change since the start of the scheme in fact was a huge escalation of discretionary payments.

By this time the external administrative environment was also very different. Under the Conservatives between 1970 and 1974 other means-tested services had proliferated to mitigate the effects of new charges and reduced central subsidies for health and local authority services – family income support, rent and rate rebates, free prescriptions, free dental treatment and free school meals and milk. The available evidence suggests that the government was responding in an ad hoc fashion to severe domestic and international pressures rather than acting out of principle. Nevertheless, its policies had widespread effects, and in particular mandatory rent and rate rebates under the 1972 Housing Finance Act, which replaced a variety of local arrangements, brought many people within the ambit of means tests for the first time.

In these circumstances under a reforming chairman, David Donnison, the Supplementary Benefits Commission developed a fatal self-criticism which contributed to its own demise. Its call for a reassessment of its work in its 1975 annual report led via the review to the 1980 Social Security Act, which extinguished the Commission and with it a voice which to some extent had been independent of the government of the day. In 1975 the recognition that many claimants on supplementary benefit would have been better-off receiving rent rebates, and vice versa, had caused particular dismay, but this had only seemed symptomatic of a far wider incoherence. By 1980 Donnison believed that the whole scheme would collapse if the three million claiming supplementary benefits, and possibly another million entitled to do so, were to ask for everything to which they might be entitled.

A huge increase in discretionary payments had also contributed to self-criticism by creating an impression of arbitrariness and by encouraging administrative decisions to be challenged. The 1966 Act had been intended to reduce discretion so that claimants might grasp more easily what their rights were; and for a few years a sharp drop occurred in exceptional circumstances allowances and exceptional needs additions, the two forms of discretionary payment which had been inherited from national assistance. In 1971, however, this trend reversed. By the middle of the decade almost half of claimants were receiving one or other payment, and in another 5 per cent or so of cases the exercise of discretion was reducing benefits. 'Exceptions' had become the norm. The new trend was a response to the growing number and diversity of claims. It could not be taken, however, as proof of the scheme's adaptability and effectiveness, since appeals against decisions were also rising, and many claimants were still living in deprived circumstances. In 1976, for example, despite the existence of discretionary grants for clothing the children of three-quarters of unemployed claimants were found to lack the minimum clothing as defined in the regulations.

The 1980 Act aimed to restore administrative control, to eliminate anomalies, to simplify, yet again, the regulations, and to do so essentially by minimalizing the role of discretion. The ban on any increased spending effectively limited what could be done to little else. The review had argued that the extent of the scheme largely explained its weakness, but any substantial shift of responsibility away from it was ruled out, because any alternative would have been more expensive. Only some internal redirection of existing spending was possible, and since the hardening of the system left the Supplementary Benefits Commission without any executive functions, its extinction became inevitable.

During these two decades of change in the 1960s and 1970s a third and final development, the reform of local health and welfare services, also contributed to the new balance of policy and social administration that had emerged before the Conservatives won the 1979 election. In this instance the same disillusionment with postwar legislation – a sense that needs had either been left uncovered or were not being fully met – became evident as in the cases of national insurance and national assistance. If anything, this happened earlier, though concern always remained more narrowly confined, mainly to voluntary organizations and professional groups outside the political mainstream. The changes in this area were not marginal, however, and contributed as much as those in the other two to the refocusing and redirection of general policy.

The town and county councils had lost control over public hospitals in 1946 and 1947 and responsibility for the remnants of local public assistance in 1948. They retained, however, a substantial role, which was either new or had been redefined, in the provision of health and social welfare. Dissatisfaction arose almost at once simply from the perception that this reorganization had not gone far enough, and that a more fundamental one was necessary. In 1948 there were immediate complaints that the Children's Act was wrong to leave neglected children outside institutions to the care of voluntary societies. Councils were also soon being accused of exercising their general responsibilities haphazardly, with what justice is difficult to say since, though standards varied widely, total spending was rising. Much of this criticism came from social workers, who were becoming increasingly professionalized. The Younghusband inquiry on their role and training accepted in 1959 that they had a common identity and dismissed the different administrative settings in which they worked as imposing unreal divisions; and in 1962 the Standing Conference of Organisations of Social Workers (the forerunner of the British Association of Social Workers) was established, just as the debate on local services entered a new phase with the Ingleby and Kilbrandon inquiries.

Both Committees were appointed to consider legal and other measures for dealing with children and young people in need or in trouble before the courts, and separate inquiries were necessary because of differences between English and Scots law. However, Ingleby proved to be far less radical than Kilbrandon. It proposed that in England and Wales legal and administrative action should be coordinated through case conferences or joint meetings, leaving the existing law and framework of services virtually untouched. In contrast for Scotland Kilbrandon proposed to take children outside the courts, at least in the first instance, by creating lay panels to deal with previous categories of offence and to create what it called a 'matching field organizations', a director of social education and his staff, within existing education departments.

Kilbrandon's recommendations were carried further on the advice of three expert advisors appointed by the Scottish Office (of whom Titmuss was one), in consultations with local authorities and professional groups. Lay or children's panels were preserved, and the proposed social education department enlarged into an independent social work department, bringing together social workers from different parts of local government, with powers to deal not only with the health, welfare and probation of children but also with family and community needs. The Ingleby Report had been so disappointing because it had been widely expected to recommend a major administrative shake-up which would lead to some sort of family service of this kind. Indeed pressure for one was so strong that Titmuss and others started to warn that the aim must be to meet a much wider diversity of needs in the local community. The result in the end was the appointment of the Seebohm Committee to re-examine the issues for England and Wales with a remit, to consider 'local authority and allied personal services', that echoed Beveridge's in 1941. But its scope was narrower than it seemed, since housing policy as a whole, probation, the operation of national assistance and changes in central government to match those at the local level were explicitly ruled out of bounds by its terms of reference.

After two and a half years the Committee reported in 1968, just as the Social Work (Scotland) Act carried the revised Kilbrandon recommendations into law. Its recommendations for local departments similar to the new Scottish ones were carried into force by the 1970 Local Authority Social Services Act, despite the Secretary of State for Health and Social Services, Richard Crossman, privately describing the Report as the most boring and unconvincing document he had ever read. His comment in his diary encapsulated the lack of political interest (except when ministerial jealousies were aroused). The resulting vacuum was filled by the lobbying of the legal, medical and social-work professions, and as a study of pressure-group activity Hall's account of the Seebohm Committee and the 1970 Act rivals Gilbert's account of the creation of health insurance. In this struggle the social-work lobby proved much more effective because it had such clear and radical proposals. In contrast the medical profession's attempt to maintain existing administrative divisions, and the Medical Officer of Health's prominence within local government, contradicted the logic of the Committee's appointment by denying that fundamental changes were necessary. The issue in the end became simply the need to define the new social service department's boundaries with the education and health services, and it was settled in consultations between ministers and civil servants and representatives of the Standing Conference.

The 1970 Act created what at the time was frequently called a 'fifth social service'.[18] The most notable sceptic of its value was Townsend, who argued that reform had proceeded from the wrong starting-point of administrative weaknesses instead of social objectives, and he and a few others criticized what they saw as Seebohm's vagueness in failing to estimate the extent of unmet needs or to define the aims of the new service. However, his own definition of what its aims should be – the equalization of resources, the reduction of isolation, support for the family and community integration – was so general that it was not at odds with Seebohm's tenor at least. A more valid point perhaps was made by Crossman, when he complained that the cost of implementing the Seebohm recommendations had not been considered. It is difficult to see, however, that the Committee could have settled either the priorities of the new service or the inseparable matter of its cost, when demands on it would clearly be neither constant nor limited. Rising unemployment and other pressures on families and communities soon reconciled Seebohm's supporters and critics, as expectations that the new service would be able to do much more than cope with poverty and mitigate its effects were quickly disappointed. On the tenth anniversary of the Report's publication the British Association of Social Workers passed a motion at its annual conference condemning the 1970 Act for having bureaucratized social work. By this time the fifth social service was struggling to meet increasing needs with inadequate resources, even though it had become, after education, the second largest spending department within local government.

In 1979 the Conservatives therefore entered into an unenviable inheritance. The main recommendations of the supplementary benefits review were easily implemented by the new government in 1980, since their basic premise, that there should be no overall increase in cost, was not at odds with Conservative promises during the election to control public expenditure. However, the gap between intentions and effects, which the review had described, widened as spending rose despite the assertions that its reduction was a key part of economic and monetary strategy. It increased in particular because the government's initial fiscal policies pushed up unemployment as, of course, did international conditions.

Even before the announcement in 1984 by the Secretary of State for Social Services, Norman Fowler, that four teams would be set up to review benefits and pensions, and the appearance of Green and White Papers on social security the following year, it was evident that any effort to maintain the Beveridge consensus, or what remained of it, was being abandoned. At the heart of the government's policy, before and after the Fowler review, lay benefit cuts and the curtailment of national insurance. The automatic updating of insurance benefits and child allowances was first modified and then abandoned; graduation ended in the case of sickness and unemployment benefit and was scaled down in the case of pensions; harsher requirements narrowed eligibility; and the introduction of income support in 1988 was accompanied by the imposition of a strict budgetary ceiling. These restrictions were not always acknowledged to be desirable and were sometimes only presented as inevitable in the current economic climate. It was sometimes claimed, however, that lower benefits would force the unemployed to search for and to accept work – often inevitably at low pay – and such claims became especially controversial when at the same time cuts in the higher rates of income tax were also being justified on the grounds that they were necessary to maintain incentives. The strange psychological implication appeared to be, as J. K. Galbraith pointed out, that the poor did not work because they had too much money, the rich because they had too little, and in his study of poverty and incentives Richard Hemming concluded that virtually any relationship between them which was postulated, could be supported by a particular set of economic data.[20]

In some instances reductions might be defended as a rationalization of means-tested support. Following the Fowler review, the 1986 Social Security Act replaced supplementary benefit by income support and family income support by family credit, and a common assessment, based on calculating net income after tax and national insurance deductions, was introduced for housing benefit and for the two renamed benefits. However, though some anomalies were cleared up (which had been created by the government's earlier legislation as well as inherited), a poverty trap remained. This was set by means-tested support, heavier insurance contributions, low pay and low tax thresholds, and it could be triggered either by entry into employment or by wage rises, either of which might end eligibility for benefits and lead to a net loss of income. An unemployment trap, which penalized the acceptance of work, can be distinguished from a trap of low pay, since only the second was affected by fiscal drag or the failure of income tax thresholds and allowances to rise in line with inflation and earnings. But however the trap is described, it was widening with the expansion of the different forms of means-tested income support.

The extent to which the Heath government had intended to move decisively away from universalism may be uncertain, but a decade later there could be no doubting the course that policy was taking. The government's 'attack on national insurance', as Michael Hill has called it, started with the abolition of earnings-related additions to sickness and unemployment benefit in 1980 and proceeded on a wide front. In 1982 sickness benefit was replaced by statutory sick pay (paid by employers who were reimbursed by rebates on their insurance contributions). Maternity benefit was removed in a similar way, and funeral benefit also disappeared. State earnings-related pensions survived, but in a much reduced form, with incentives offered to move to private schemes and more of the cost loaded on to contributions. Finally, in 1988 the principle of a Treasury contribution to the Insurance Fund was formally abandoned. National insurance was rapidly 'losing its centrality' as the Conservative attack was pressed home.[21] By 1988 unemployment was still covered, though many of the unemployed were disqualified, and invalidity benefit still replaced sick pay when the right to it ended after six months. Sickness and maternity benefit remained, but only for a very small minority of contributors, who were qualified by recent contributions but not in employment at the time of their entitlement. In one respect, however, there was no change. Contributions were not being scaled down in line with benefits, in fact the reverse was happening, and more openly than ever before the scheme was a system of taxation.

The attack, of course, had been mounted on a weakened position. In 1982, when sick pay became the responsibility of employers, about 80 per cent of the working population was covered by private occupational arrangements, and as a result of the 1966 Act's limitation of the duration of claims to a year and its barriers to requalification only one million out of the 2.8 million unemployed – recorded officially in a way which was about to change – were on insurance benefit. Nevertheless, until the attack started, national insurance, along with children's allowances, full employment and the National Health Service, was still one of the four pillars of universalism, and very little of it remained standing afterwards.

After 1979 the Conservative governments, which held power for an unprecedented long and continuous period, no doubt broke with the past. But this statement raises two questions, neither of which is all that easily answered – what past, and what was the nature of the break? Much of the postwar legislation and its underlying certainties had already gone, and it is debatable whether Thatcherism can be defined as an ideology which aimed to destroy what remained. The new Conservatism's exaltation of market forces and minimal government and its attack on high taxation, social spending and personal dependency were new, though foreshadowed in neo-liberal or new-right thinking and occasionally in party rhetoric in opposition. However, the influence of Hayek or Friedman after 1979 cannot be traced in the same way as that of Beveridge, Keynes or Titmuss earlier. Throughout the 1980s economic and social policies seem not so much grounded on any firm theoretical or ideological bases as shifting in response to changing pressures, and even the reduction of direct taxation, which supplied an element of consistency, seems populist and a matter of electoral calculation rather than anything else. The priority given to controlling inflation was justified initially by monetary theories but these were never followed consistently. As one dissident Conservative put it, 'Thatcherism can be viewed as ideology, style, mood'.[19] In other words, its only real consistency was its capacity to be at one and the same time both dogmatic and anti-intellectual.

Notes

1 *Social Insurance, The Government Scheme*, 1943–4 (Cmnd 6550).
2 Ibid., p. 7.
3 W. A. Robson (ed.), *Social Security* (1944).
4 On the Beveridge Report's genesis and reception Alan Bullock, *Life and Times of Ernest Bevin*, Vol. II (1967) was written before cabinet and departmental papers were open to consultation but is still valuable. Among the accounts written since Jose Harris, *William Beveridge* (1977) and Alec Cairncross and Nita Watts, *The Economic Section, 1939–1961* (1989) are perhaps the ones of most obvious use or value.
5 Arthur Marwick, 'Middle Opinion in the 'Thirties: Planning

Progress and Political Agreement', *English Historical Review*, lxxix (1964); also J. Pinder (ed.), *Fifty Years of Social and Economic Planning* (1981), and Alan Booth and Melvyn Pack, *Employment, Capital and Economic Policy* (1985).

6 Janet Beveridge, *Beveridge and his Plan* (1954), chapter VI.

7 Alan Deacon, 'Coercion and Concialiation: The Politics of Unemployment in the 1920s', in A. Briggs and J. Saville (eds), *Essays in Labour History, II* (1977), and *In Search of the Scrounger: The Administration of Unemployment Insurance in Great Britain, 1920–31* (1976).

8 Paul Addison, *The Road to 1945* (1975).

9 Alec Cairncross, *Years of Recovery: British Economic Policy, 1945–51* (1985); Elizabeth Durbin, *New Jerusalems: The Labour Party and the Economics of Democratic Socialism* (1985).

10 Peter Hall (ed.), *Labour's New Frontiers* (1964).

11 Elizabeth Wilson, *Women and the Welfare State* (1977); Hilary Land, 'The Family Wage', *Feminist Review* (1980).

12 Peter Townsend, *Poverty in the United Kingdom* (1979); see also Wilfrid Beckermann and Stephen Clark, *Poverty and Social Security in Britain since 1961* (1982).

13 Olive Stevenson, *Claimant or Client?* (1973).

14 R. M. Titmuss, *Social Policy* (1974), chapter 8.

15 This is the description by A. W. Dilnot, J. A. Kay and C. N. Morris, *The Reform of Social Security* (1984), p. 27.

16 *Social Assistance: A Review of the Supplementary Benefits Scheme in Great Britain*, DHSS July 1978, p. 3.

17 Frank Field, *Poverty and Politics: The Inside Story of the CPAG Campaigns in the 1970s* (1982). Cf. Eric Briggs and A. M. Rees, *Supplementary Benefits and the Consumer* (1980).

18 Health, education, social security and housing counted as the other four.

19 Ian Gilmour, *Dancing with Dogma: Britain Under Thatcherism* (1992), p. 10.

20 Richard Hemming, *Poverty and Incentives* (1984) (which also quotes Galbraith's remark).

21 Michael Hill, *Social Security Policy in Great Britain* (1990), pp. 58–9.

3

Beveridge's Assumptions

The Plan in Context

Beveridge was fortunate in the timing of his inquiry. The government had already committed itself to reforming the hospital services after the Second World War, and wider changes of the entire system of public and private health care had become unavoidable. Within the Economic Section of the Cabinet Office the discussions of postwar employment policy had started that were to lead to the 1944 White Paper. A fresh debate on the need for family allowances had also started. Beveridge, of course, knew of what was going on elsewhere in Whitehall. He deserves great credit, however, for his ability to see this reconstruction planning as a whole. It was his capacity of vision which made his Report unique and gives it claims to greatness. The only precedents for such a powerful and comprehensive analysis of policy were the 1909 Majority and Minority Poor Law Reports, and they in the end do not quite measure up. Certainly no subsequent inquiry, official or unofficial, into the problems and issues with which Beveridge was concerned can bear comparison. The most recent of them by Labour's Social Justice Commission certainly cannot.

Full Employment

That governments can maintain employment at a high and stable level now seems the most striking of Beveridge's three assumptions, but this is the view from the other side, as it were, after the collapse of full employment. In 1942 it was already so widely accepted that Beveridge did not feel obliged to justify it at any length, and his explanation of its significance occupied only two pages of the Report. He was more cautious than two years later in estimating the residual unemployment which would remain under conditions of full employment, and his growing optimism did set him slightly apart from general expert opinion. By 1942, however, it was already confidently believed that the experience between the wars would not be repeated, and that employment would be kept at a high level, however this was defined.

Beveridge was not himself an expert economist. Despite pretensions to be an authority on the labour market and on the history of prices, he was uncomfortable with abstract theorizing, and in 1936 his reading of Keynes's *General Theory of Employment, Interest and Money* had left him critical and confused, disconcerted that his unfavourable opinion was not shared by economists whom he respected. Even in 1942, as Jose Harris has pointed out, 'Assumption C, the maintenance of employment', mainly reflected the influence of G. D. H. Cole and the Webbs and their belief in centralized planning. He had changed his mind only in the sense that he now believed the kind of economic management practised in the Soviet Union could be undertaken successfully within a democracy. In effect Britain was already a planned economy with rationing, compulsory savings and five million people in the armed forces or munitions industries through the direction of labour.

Beveridge's conversion to Keynesianism, if it can be called this, came later in 1943 and 1944 after his exclusion from official policy-making, when he embarked on the inquiries with led to the publication of *Full Employment in a Free Society*. Civil servants were told (in what Hugh Dalton in his diary called a 'quite Henry James' letter from Sir Richard Hopkins at the Treasury) not to give him any help, and he was dependent on private funds from a group of businessmen and on the assistance and advice of a number of youngish economists such as Nicholas Kaldor. His book in the end was a more radical statement of faith in macro-economic management of demand and investment than the government's White Paper, *Employment Policy*, which had appeared five months earlier in June 1944, and with which it was inevitably compared. Though his grasp of theoretical issues was probably as uncertain as ever, his views had been changed by his advisors, who saw themselves as Keynes's disciples. He fully acknowledged his dependence upon them, and his personal contribution seems to have been largely confined to putting their conclusions and proposals in his own style of sometimes cloudy moral rhetoric.

It is clear, however, that Beveridge's intellectual progress was not all that unusual. A similar eclecticism, though combined with far greater self-confidence, can be detected, for example, in the evolution of the views of Evan Durbin, Hugh Gaitskell and other socialists of their generation, whose careers within the Labour party were being furthered through the patronage of Cole and Dalton. They were influenced by Dennis Robertson's criticism of the *General Theory* as too static a model of economic change, which neglected long-term problems of growth and stability, and their central concern with how to achieve efficiency within a mixed economy made them want to adapt Keynesianism rather than accept it wholesale.

The character of the changes in economic policy between the early 1930s and the later 1940s has been extensively debated for at least the last 20 years. The traditional account of a Keynesian revolution in theory, in Harrod's biography and descriptions of the Cambridge 'circus' of economists who helped Keynes to reformulate his views between the publication of his *Treatise on Money* in 1930 and the *General Theory* six years later, has been restated and amplified, and its impact variously traced to the 1941 budget, which used new methods of national income accounting to monitor the economy's performance, or the 1947 one, which created a surplus to counter inflationary pressure. But this reading of the evolution of theory and practice has been challenged by two forms of revisionism. One rehabilitates Robertson, A. C. Pigou and perhaps some other critics of Keynes, or tries to do so, partly by arguing that he shared more common ground with them than his polemical temperament allowed him to admit, and it has even been suggested that the continued evolution of his thinking by the end of the 1930s was separating him from his disciples. Moderate versions of these views have been accepted in retrospect by some of those who took sides in the original controversies, but the more extreme at least can be attacked for their selective approach to Keynes's writings and for exaggerating his critics' coherence. The other form of revisionism attaches less importance to such past and present divisions of professional opinion by stressing the priority of practical considerations and the tendency of governments to use whatever theoretical justifications are at hand to explain their actions. It too devalues the influence of Keynes, but it does so partly because his self-confidence and intellectual arrogance made him less sceptical than his opponents of the power of reason in public life, and it is critical really of the capacity of any body of theory to control the short-term and specific concerns of government.

The examination of economic and financial policy certainly shows the Treasury and other departments struggling with a number of different and changing objectives during what remains undeniably a crucial period of transition. Between the wars public spending had been creeping up, and pressure on it increased in the later 1930s with rearmament. As a result by 1939 an attempt had already started to try to control aggregate demand by fiscal and other devices, though it was not being pursued along Keynsian lines. Attention was also shifting to the need to influence the location of industry in order to mop up the pools of depression which were being left behind as the economy recovered, and the 1944 White Paper committed the government to avoiding substantial regional disparities as well as to maintaining a high level of employment.

Fears of the inflationary consequences of these commitments strengthened the concern to keep public expenditure in check. In fact Keynesian demand management appears to have become acceptable to Treasury officials partly because they preferred it as a means of controlling inflation to the continued use of the price controls and food subsidies which had been introduced during the war. Since subsidies pushed up spending, the Treasury wanted to abolish them as quickly as possible, and their survival was due paradoxically to the inability of Labour Chancellors of the Exchequer to impose an effective ceiling on public expenditure between 1947 and 1951. This failure led the government to turn to voluntary wage restraint as a means of curbing it and to the retention of food subsidies in order to increase the chances of success for this new policy. Subsidies were finally phased out after the Conservatives returned to power, but by this time the attempt at wage restraint had been abandoned, the inflation rate had slackened, and the anomaly of having a prices without a wages policy had been recognized by the Labour government before it lost the election.

How the transformation is described appears to be partly a matter of semantics. The 1944 White Paper can be seen as a compromise between Keynesian and Treasury concerns, depending on how both are defined, but no serious divisions existed over its final version. The first drafts were written within the Economic Section by James Meade, a former member of the Cambridge 'circus', and revised by Sir Richard Hopkins, the Treasury's Permanent Secretary in the light of various criticisms and suggestions. Greater space as a result was given to the impact of international conditions, to the difficulties of managing investment and dealing with regional inequalities, and especially to the connection between the level of employment and the stability of wages and prices. The final version can be called a qualified victory for the Economic Section, since the main focus of attention remained the control of investment and consumption, even if budget deficits for this purpose were not explicitly sanctioned. On the whole, however, the changes seem to have been of emphasis as much as substance.

When Beveridge's *Full Employment* was published, Meade

wrote a commentary on it for ministers, which stressed its striking similarity to the White Paper. He pointed out that there was agreement in three main areas of policy – the maintenance of adequate total outlay, control of the location of industry and securing the mobility of labour – and only his description of the first as crucial and the others as mopping-up operations seems particularly Keynesian. Even so his detailed analysis recognized that regional industrial development, moderate wage settlements, the free movement of workers and the modification of restrictive practices had all some autonomous importance. He also felt that Beveridge's proposals suffered from a perfectionism which at times amounted to a lack of realism. The White Paper had accepted that private investment and the balance of trade were both likely to fluctuate considerably. Beveridge in contrast proposed to avoid any undesirable variation at all in the former by establishing a National Investment Board with very wide powers. Meade insisted that this difference was not simply a matter of administrative machinery but represented a failure on Beveridge's part to grasp the difficulty of controlling closely not only private but also public investment by local authorities and central government. He reinforced his criticism by describing the treatment of international considerations as the least satisfactory aspect of the book.

The final matter of agreement, as Meade pointed out, was that full employment did not depend either upon maintaining private enterprise or upon nationalization. Instead he identified as vital both the need for a quick response to economic fluctuations and continuity of policy.[1] All the elements of the postwar consensus in fact seem already to be in place in his commentary: a statement of attainable and compatible economic and industrial objectives, though the priority given to each might vary; a description of the means of realizing them, despite some uncertainty about the precise degree of success to be expected; and finally confidence that political divisions would not be disruptive.

Over the next 20 years or so successive Labour and Conservative administrations conformed to this implicit model of good government, as the White Paper's policies apparently worked in practice even more successfully than had been forecast. In 1944 Beveridge had assumed that unemployment could be kept below 3 per cent. At the time this target had looked extremely optimistic, but from 1948 to 1966 the annual average was only 1.7 per cent. Afterwards it began to creep up slowly until a decade later, between 1976 and 1979, it was averaging 5.9 per cent. By this time full employment appeared to be collapsing, but this judgement reflected what had come to seem normal during the previous 30 years rather than expectations at the end of the war. The White Paper had cautiously not specified any target, but most experts had believed that, once its policies were in force, the residue of unemployment would be between 5 and 8 per cent. Not until the 1980s did the level greatly exceed this higher figure, by how much is difficult to say because of changes in the methods of recording the numbers out of work, apparently made more to disguise their full seriousness than in the interests of greater accuracy.

In a famous article in 1968 R. C. O. Matthews argued that full employment was an aspect of the long international boom after the Second World War rather than a result of government policy.[2] Certainly economic management, whether a subsidiary factor or not, was being pursued in circumstances which were extremely favourable to its aims for more than 20 years after 1945. Just as it had after the end of the First World War, the economy immediately expanded because of stock-building and consumer spending, but this time the initial boom, far from petering out, was sustained by the strength of private and public investment, demands for British exports, low interest rates, technical and administrative innovations and the prolonged worldwide economic expansion. There was nothing unique about the British experience. Disagreement arises, however, not only over the role of government during this period but also over the explanation for the comparatively low growth and productivity which differentiated Britain from her main European competitors.

These issues, unfortunately or not, cannot be completely

separated from the theoretical controversies which broke out as the boom faded. Monetarist claims that Keynesianism was irrelevant at best, harmful at worst, during the years of growing prosperity when it constituted a powerful orthodoxy, have been answered in various ways, some more defensive in tone than others. Postwar policies can be seen as having made a positive contribution to maintaining growth and high employment, and their gradual abandonment as having worsened the stagnation of the British economy. The alternative view is that the failure to control public expenditure and the neglect of money supply considerations, by pushing up prices and weakening industrial efficiency and competitiveness, contributed to Britain's difficulties. Even its supporters can admit that Keynesianism was ill-equipped theoretically to deal with the unprecedented combination of low growth and high inflation during the 1970s, and needed some reformulation to cope, though these concessions stop well short of accepting the validity of its displacement. The most uncompromising defence, as well as the one with the longest historical perspective, was Nicholas Kaldor's. He saw governments in the 1920s and the 1980s as labouring under the same mistaken dogma: the return to the Gold Standard in 1926 under the influence of the Cunliffe Report caused positive harm, and the long theoretical retreat from the Radcliffe Committee's refusal to endorse monetarist policies in 1959 reproduced in the end the same undesirable effects, which had been eliminated by the Gold Standard's forced abandonment in September 1931 and the sharp reduction in the Bank rate that followed from this, well before Keynes supplied a theoretical justification for the change of direction.[3]

Virtually only two or perhaps three points, which are related rather than separate, seem beyond dispute. The first is that full employment as a prime objective had been abandoned before the 1979 election, when the Conservatives insisted that controlling inflation must have a higher priority. Labour's spending cuts between 1975 and 1978 had doubled the numbers out of work and imposed restrictions upon the social services that weakened confidence in their effectiveness just as they were coming under greater pressure. The psychological effects are impossible to measure, but the commitment to full employment had lasted for so long that its abandonment inevitably cast doubt on whether other objectives of the postwar consensus could be maintained. Callaghan's speech to a hostile Labour conference in 1976, insisting that it was no longer possible to hold that a government could spend its way out of a depression, did not spell out what the consequences might be, if this were true. But clearly enough one implication was that the level of economic activity necessary to support high spending on good public services could not be sustained.

However, the second point, which became very clear after 1979, was that heavy unemployment imposed a dual strain on public expenditure. Substantial payments to those out of work, despite benefit cuts, were matched by a loss of revenue from income tax and national insurance, despite contribution increases. Monetarism postulated that unregulated markets would produce jobs, if not in the short at least in the medium term, and like pre-Keynesian theory represented a high level of employment as a point of natural equilibrium. The Conservative poster during the 1979 election of the huge dole queue, winding into the distance, above the words, 'Labour isn't working', was an indirect promise that demand would expand, as well as an attempt to capitalize on anxiety. In fact monetarist theory failed in practice with predictable consequences. With far more people not working under the Conservatives public expenditure was pushed up as the tax base narrowed, in exactly the way Beveridge in 1942 had described would happen, in the course of arguing that full employment was a prerequisite for an adequate system of social security.

In these circumstances the political dialogue lost much of its coherence. Beveridge had described productive work as necessary for personal happiness, and experience during the 1980s perhaps showed this to be true. Opinion polls certainly revealed a general sense of both personal insecurity and alarm over the possible damage which was being inflicted on the social fabric. Conservative ministers did not consistently deny the strains imposed on individuals and families, even on society as a whole, and usually insisted only on the absence of any alternative to their own fiscal and economic strategies in existing international conditions. There was little disagreement that it was impossible within the foreseeable future to get back to the very low levels of unemployment which had prevailed for 20 or 30 years after 1945. But opinion was bitterly divided over the extent to which the government's inaction as well as its policies had pushed unemployment beyond what was unavoidable, and over what the social consequences might be, if it remained so high. Four election victories gave the Conservatives not the best of the argument but the last word. It was not that the two sides were further apart than before. The Labour party in fact had as much difficulty moving off as fighting on the ground chosen by its opponents. The decline of Keynesianism, however, removed any shared sense of the balance which was necessary to survive politically and to manage the economy successfully, as the old tactical considerations, especially the belief in a trade-off between unemployment and electoral popularity, disappeared along with any clear theoretical orthodoxy. The postwar consensus had been a matter of accepting limits within which decisions had to be taken as much as anything else, and once the assumption of full employment disappeared, so did any agreed set of options or recognized boundaries to disagreement.

The National Health Service

The second major assumption in the 1942 Report was that a 'satisfactory scheme of social security' depended upon 'comprehensive health and rehabilitation services for prevention and cure of disease and restoration of the capacity to work' being 'available to all members of the community'.[4] Its history is free from the controversy which clouds historical debate on full employment. The three accounts of the creation of the National Health Service, written since the opening of the Cabinet and departmental papers, differ only on points of detail or emphasis. The earliest is by a former civil servant,

J. E. Pater, who had played a part in the events he describes; and what might be called its quasi-official status is reinforced by its publication by the King Edward's Hospital Fund. The second is the official account, Charles Webster's volume in the Peacetime History of British Government since the Second World War. Its critical rather than descriptive approach makes it less like the volume in the War History on civilian health and medical services by McNalty, which appeared in 1953, than Titmuss's *Problems of Social Policy* in the earlier series; but even so it amplifies essentially the known record. The third account by Honigsbaum surveys much the same ground, concentrating in a similar way on civil service planning and the reactions of the medical profession to it.

While previous writing has been superseded, the same is not true of older explanations. Medical history, especially when written by doctors, tends to emphasize gradual progress based on agreement to use scientific knowledge as effectively as possible. James Stirling Ross's 'historical and descriptive' study of the National Health Service, published in 1952, exemplifies this approach; and both Pater and Webster – like him – open with surveys of interwar proposals for reform. Honigsbaum only differs by taking up this debate at a later starting point in the 1930s. Pater even suggests that the National Health Service's creation can be resolved into the story of the delayed implementation of the Dawson Report, which in 1920 had proposed the integration of all medical care, from general practice to the most prestigious hospitals, into a system of primary, secondary and tertiary medical centres. This judgement largely ignores the diversity, uncertainty and changing character of opinion within the medical profession and elsewhere, not just on the Report but also other issues; and Webster concludes that the tendency to see the National Health Service's creation as an act of consensus is only supported to a moderate extent by the evidence. His concentration on the deliberations of successive Coalition, Labour and Conservative ministers and their civil servants, however, leads to a centralist approach, which makes relatively minor reservations to the theme of continuity and places

in the background issues such as the neglect of mental illness during planning (despite the fact that in 1946 most
hospital beds were in asylums). Its advantage is that it allows
the activities of pressure groups to be seen in a proper context. Honigsbaum's starting point is the 1936 Cathcart
Report's attempt to reconcile divergent municipal and
medical interests, and his assessment of the National Health
Service as a compromise between the high ideals of civil servants and medical politics provides another variation on the
theme of consensus.

The NHS's origins undoubtedly lie in the transformation
during the Second World War of a debate which had been
going on virtually since the end of the First World War. What
seems less certain is the degree of continuity, and also the
extent to which planning reflected wide agreement. The
establishment of the National Health Service in 1948 can be
seen as a remarkably altruistic act, and its subsequent operation has sometimes been invested with a great moral authority. This view was most clearly stated by Titmuss in his study
of blood donorship, *The Gift Relationship*, which linked the
effectiveness of the non-commercial National Blood Transfu-
sion Service in Britain to the wider values of the whole Health
Service, and it was also expressed in some of his other writing.
It obviously implies, without dealing directly with previous
medical services, that 1948 marked a break with the past in a
way which is at odds with the stress on continuity.

The state of play just before the Second World War was
summed up in the deliberations of a small group of civil servants within the Ministry of Health that was brought together
in 1938 to consider possible future developments. At its first
meeting Sir John Maude, the Permanent Secretary, identified
two ways forward, either through the extension of national
health insurance, by widening its cover and introducing new
statutory benefits, or through the development of local
authority provisions. Neither offered, however, a satisfactory
route towards a national hospital service, which was seen as
the most pressing need, and Sir Arthur MacNalty, the Chief
Medical Officer, argued that the Ministry itself must take

responsibility for setting up and supervising regional boards, with the duty of planning and coordinating the work of both municipal and voluntary hospitals.

During the early stages of the war it was this problem which continued to attract attention. The creation of the Emergency Hospital Service brought a national system into existence without resolving the long-standing antagonism between the public and private sectors that before 1939 had prevented them from co-operating. In 1937 the Sankey Commission, set up by the British Hospitals Association which represented the voluntary interests, had recommended that private hospitals should be grouped on a regional basis as part of a wider rationalization. The extent to which the voluntary lobby was willing to sacrifice its autonomy, however, remained unclear. Relations between it and the local authorities were marked by mutual dislike and suspicion, which only deepened after the Nuffield Provincial Hospital Trust was established in 1939 with the aim of helping forward the process of regional planning. The Trust identified as the main priority the enforcement of local consultation and argued that town and county councils had been flouting their obligation to consult voluntary hospitals under the 1929 Local Government Acts, that the financial difficulties of the charitable sector had worsened as a result, and that in future there must be cooperation. Whatever their validity, such arguments did not promote reconciliation.

The Ministry of Health could scarcely disagree that the law should be observed. But already by 1941 its civil servants felt that regionalization implied the further decline of the voluntary sector and the continued expansion of local authority hospital provisions. In October Ernest Brown, the Minister, announced that the government was committed to establishing a free and comprehensive hospital service after the war, but this low-key statement only served to postpone awkward decisions, and in England no real consideration was given to what it meant until 1943. Detailed planning started in Scotland, however, on the assumption, which reflected the prevailing state of informed opinion, that local authorities would have statutory responsibility for a regional service, with voluntary hospitals having a protected but subordinate status.

The Beveridge Report not only revived discussion in England but also shifted its focus. It did so despite containing nothing about the form of the new service which would provide comprehensive care for all. This was partly because Beveridge had been persuaded to stay silent. However, it was scarcely necessary for him to state anything in detail, since the bare assumption was sufficient to widen planning to include the future of general practice.

Before the war the BMA had accepted that the cover of national health insurance should be extended and the treatment available under it improved. At first this issue had been caught up in negotiations over a revised capitation fee, when the contract for panel service came up for renewal, but gradually it had come to be considered in a more general, if not necessarily disinterested way. Particularly in the 1930s the expansion of hospital and local authority medical services was squeezing general practice and concentrating the BMA's mind on its future. The Association's blueprint for reform, *A General Medical Service for the Nation*, issued in 1930 and revised in 1938, was to some extent preemptive. It advocated the extension of medical benefit to the dependants of contributors, but a largely rhetorical attachment to private practice held the Association back from any further commitments, and the disadvantage of caution became painfully obvious after the outbreak of the war, when in health insurance the income limit for non-manual workers was raised from £250 a year to £450, even though the change was essentially intended to take account of inflation.

Many doctors in fact were coming round to accepting the inevitability of the so-called '90 per cent solution' – an extension of health insurance so great that private practice would become narrowly confined to the highest income groups. In 1942 this was the view taken in its *Draft Interim Report* by the BMA's Medical Planning Committee, which was set up to examine the war's impact on future health care; and the Committee also showed a progressive enthusiasm for the creation of health centres as a means of improving standards. Webster describes the Report as liberal, disjointed and unrepresentative, but also influential, particularly in encouraging both Beveridge and civil servants at the Ministry of Health to face the need to reconstruct general health rather than only hospital services. The BMA's problem was always to reconcile its desire to improve the quality of care with the financial and professional interests of its members, and the *Interim Report* showed how difficult it was at times to strike a balance. For many GPs the prospect of moving into health centres, better equipped than private surgeries, with colleagues on hand for consultation, and with some degree of specialization possible, despite its attractions was profoundly disturbing, because they equated it with a loss of professional autonomy and the introduction of a salaried service under local authority control.

Evidence to Beveridge's Committee often raised wider issues than the future of health insurance, and this influenced his thinking, though he agreed not to publish his conclusions. In particular he apparently became convinced that the panel system should be replaced by a community medical service, and was persuaded to stay silent by Ministry of Health civil servants, who realized how controversial this proposal would be, and how strongly the BMA would resist it. Despite this, when they were forced into action themselves by the imminence of the Beveridge Report's publication, their planning guidelines included the establishment of a full-time salaried service for general practitioners, working in health centres. They had persuaded themselves that this proposal could be made acceptable to the BMA by creating a 'Central Medical Board', which would determine salaries and conditions of service. Their other major decision was to reject the '90 per cent' solution in favour of comprehensive cover of the whole population on the grounds that it would be difficult and valueless to draw up criteria for exclusion.

When negotiations with the BMA started in January 1943, civil servants expected to move quickly towards the publication of a White Paper and then legislation. Hopes of agreement, however, almost at once collapsed. The BMA leadership proved to be violently hostile to the Ministry's plans, and though consultations were supposed to be confidential, much of the acrimony became public in speeches and leaks to the press. About the same time the appearance of the Scottish Heatherington Report, proposing to end hospital insurance schemes and the assessment and recovery of costs from hospital patients, alarmed the voluntary hospital lobby and divided Ministers. The publication of a White Paper on the new health service as a result was delayed until February 1944, and even when it eventually appeared, its compromises reflected a loss of confidence rather than agreement.

Nevertheless, differences never became clear-cut. Coalition ministers were divided over whether the panel system should be retained or superseded, but many practical issues, such as the need to direct newly qualified GPs into districts where they were most required, did not depend on any particular set of administrative arrangements for their resolution. Though the White Paper ruled out a full change to a salaried service, it proposed that health centres should be given a large-scale trial alongside modified panel practice; and a poll of BMA members from a 48 per cent response found 53 per cent against and 39 per cent in favour of these proposals. Similar uncertainty surrounded the proposals for Regional Hospital Advisory Councils, with equal local authority and voluntary hospital representation, and beneath them Joint Boards to exercise direct administrative control over hospitals. In the Coalition Cabinet Herbert Morrison, who had risen to national prominence from London politics, argued that joint authorities never worked (though later as a Labour Minister he came to defend them in an attempt to preserve municipal responsibility from even greater erosion). The voluntary hospital lobby was just as unenthusiastic about the proposed administration. In these circumstances the White Paper's appearance barely interrupted negotiations. Only after its publication did the BMA abandon the idea of '90 per cent' cover, and the government any idea of a salaried service (which whittled health centres down into a limited experiment). There was still no final agreement, because by this time the BMA leaders, just as in 1911, had hemmed themselves into a generalized opposition, but an outline Bill, which the caretaker Conservative government decided not to publish, was ready before the 1945 election.

Aneurin Bevan, the new Labour Minister of Health, acted quickly and decisively to break the deadlock, largely along lines which were already obvious, despite the protests he provoked. He decided on a tripartite administration for the National Health Service, with local authorities responsible for their existing clinics and the new health centres, separate panel practice with little changed except names from health insurance, and the nationalization of hospitals with both the local authorities and private boards of trustees losing control over the institutions which they had previously owned and managed. Though health centres were allocated to town and county councils, the new Executive (or old Insurance) Committees became responsible for the contracts of the doctors employed there. Continuity was greatest in general practice, and the inclusion of dental and opthalmic treatment – another issue on which Bevan acted decisively to end uncertainty – was achieved on the basis of the model provided by panel service. Hardly any health centres were built until the end of the 1960s, but mainly because they had such a low priority in central government policy, and once local authorities received incentives to provide them, and GPs financial and other inducements to move into them, they quickly started to appear.

Bevan's most striking achievement undoubtedly was to make nationalization acceptable to hospital consultants by concessions on their right to continue private practice and by giving teaching hospitals a special status. Their consciousness of the advantages of public funding, however, meant that they were more than eager to meet him half-way. In 1946, when the Conservatives in the Commons were moving the rejection of the National Health Service Bill for England and Wales during its third reading, on the grounds that it was destroying local democracy and increasing central power,

Lord Moran, the President of the English Royal College of Surgeons, in the upper house was speaking eloquently on its benefits.

Even after the Act became law the BMA still threatened to withhold its members' cooperation, but as in 1912 they were divided, and as then the dispute became in the end simply a matter of money. The Spens inquiry had assessed the future income from private general practice as negligible and awarded an interim capitation fee that the government at first insisted was ruled out by the precarious state of the economy. A higher offer, and Bevan's agreement to Moran's suggestion that there should be further legislation ruling out any salaried service, finally resolved the simmering crisis or stalemate. Anything of substance apart from remuneration had been conceded or settled years earlier, and the 1949 Amending Act had scarcely even a symbolic importance.

The creation of the NHS can be seen as a triumph over selfish sectional interests as Michael Foot presents it with great eloquence in his biography of Bevan. What came to be seen, however, as its main characteristic, that it was entirely free to patients, during its planning had never been controversial and only occasionally even a matter of peripheral consideration. (The possibility of charging for stays in hospital, for example, had been raised only to be ruled out as at odds with the ending of private hospital insurance schemes and charges.) It was always obvious that funding on the scale required had to come almost entirely from taxation, and, as Beveridge pointed out, the service was only free in the sense that what patients received for nothing, they paid for as taxpayers.

Cost only became an issue after the provisional estimates of how much it would take to run the new service rapidly proved to have been badly mistaken. Beveridge in 1942 had projected that £130 million annually would be needed at first, less in real terms as the nation's health gradually improved. The White Paper had come up with a lower figure, but by 1946 official estimates had been revised upwards to slightly above Beveridge's. In fact in 1948-9 gross expenditure proved to be running at £300 million, and supplementary estimates had to be quickly voted through parliament. Within the Cabinet and elsewhere the miscalculation could be seen, according to different considerations, as either grave or not at all serious. Bevan believed that the unexpectedly high spending arose from recent pay awards and a backlog of unmet needs and would soon come under control. Morrison raised the spectre of the 1931 financial crisis which had brought down the last Labour government. How other ministers reacted depended to some extent on their view of the general state of the economy, and later also on how serious they felt the financial impact of the Korean War was likely to be. Proposals to impose a ceiling on future NHS spending, to cut or suspend parts of the service, or to introduce charges confused and divided them. A bitter feud developed between Gaitskell and Bevan, starting before Gaitskell had succeeded Cripps as Chancellor of the Exchequer, continuing after Bevan had moved from the Ministry of Health to Transport, and culminating with Bevan's resignation when dental, opthalmic and prescription charges were introduced, as a temporary expedient, shortly before Labour lost the 1951 election.

The situation was finally clarified, on balance in Bevan's favour, by the Guillebaud Report in 1956. This Committee had been appointed by the new Conservative government, and though the initial intention had been that it should find ways of making savings, on reconsideration it had been given the less specific remit of inquiring into the cost of the Health Service. Its findings, based on research by Abel-Smith and Titmuss, showed that there was no crisis and no extravagance. By looking at expenditure as a proportion of the gross national product, and by taking into account changes in the value of money and in the population's size and age structure, they demonstrated that over the first four years cost as a share of the GNP had fallen, in real terms had risen only slightly, and per head of population had remained steady.

The Guillebaud Report also pointed to deficiencies in the Service and to a worrying decline in capital expenditure as part of the total budget. Over the next 20 years or so improvements, which were universally acknowledged to be necessary, started to be made on the basis of the agreement which had been re-established by the Report. The NHS's labour-intensive character made for difficult and expensive pay settlements, and hospital building and the application of medical advances to patient care also pushed up spending. Alarm was damped down, however, by continued economic growth, and if better provisions at an affordable cost were ever regarded as a problem, the solution of greater administrative efficiency could always be advanced. Throughout the 1960s and into the next decade the twin aims of improved services and management were pursued in Green and White Papers by Conservative and Labour Ministers of Health – Powell, Robinson, Crossman and Joseph – who raised the status of their department and acquired, at least during their period in office, a reputation as constructive and influential politicians. The Porrit Report in 1962 united the medical profession behind the abolition of tripartite administration and the transfer of all local responsibility to area health boards; and unification, though not quite on such simple lines, came in 1974 and was later modified in minor respects. More professional management was seen as the corollary of administrative reorganization; and the 1966 Salmon Report, which created a new hierarchy of nursing grades, had a significance beyond its immediate area of concern because of its use of business management as the model for reform.

It is difficult to evaluate this phase, before and after the 1974 restructuring. The policies of administrative rationalization were formulated at a time of relative optimism but implemented in a deteriorating economic situation. In these circumstances what one commentator has called 'the politics of technocratic change' gave way to 'the politics of disillusionment'.[5] Existing policies, however, only appeared to gain in relevance as financial constraints increased. Whether they were ever right is another matter. Using his expertise as a political scientist as well as his experience as a life-long patient, W. J. M. Mackenzie criticized the application of management theory to the NHS's problems and was especially contemptuous of the Salmon Report. Similarly Brian Watkin concluded his history of this 'first phase' by condemning the trend towards greater centralization and bureaucracy.[6]

However, public faith remained unaffected by such doubts, and the wide respect and support, which the National Health Service continued to enjoy, was noted in 1979 by a Royal Commission as one reason among others for rejecting any fundamental changes in administration or methods of finance. Its Report described the right level of spending as a metaphysical concept, insisted that financial pressures had to be accepted as normal and inevitable, and like Guillebaud a generation earlier endorsed, though not uncritically, a very favourable judgement of the Service's achievements. In very different economic circumstances, however, its conclusions could not provide the same immunity to concern over the level of expenditure, and the paperchase of inquiries and reports continued.

There was no particular point at which the pursuit of administrative and managerial change ceased to be a matter of agreement and became highly divisive. After a decade of Thatcherite government, however, this decisive shift had occurred. The encouragement of a private hospital sector, commercial in character and very different from the old voluntary one, scarcely mattered except as a symptomatic break with the past, because it remained so small and essentially parasitic. But hospital trusts opted out of local health board control, and fund-holding general practitioners threatened to recreate the fragmentation and inequality which in the 1930s had produced the vogue for regional planning. The justification, that internal markets would produce savings, always remained unconvincing. Savings were illusory, the result of hospital or ward closures, the sale of assets or other measures which worsened standards, and total spending continued to rise. This increase, frequently and misleadingly cited by Conservative ministers in answer to criticism, was mainly due to demographic factors and rises above the inflation rate of unavoidable costs. The stress on managerial efficiency only shifted resources from patient care to administration without any obvious accruing benefits.

Similar improvements in death rates to those in Britain had occurred since 1948 in other industrialized countries with very different systems of medical care, and, as the Black Committee described in detail in 1980, 'inequalities in health' had persisted under the NHS 'in a number of distinctive forms, of which the clearest and most unequivocal [was] the relationship between occupational class and mortality'.[7] Indeed, if anything, these disparities apparently had widened. The obvious need was for better community and preventive medicine and also for other action to raise the material living standards and to alter the lifestyle of many manual workers and their families, especially those on the lowest incomes. There were no sound grounds for implying, however, that private markets might have served 'working-class patients' better, or that their interests since 1911 had been sacrificed to those of 'the medical establishment', and arguing this case involved dismissing all previous well-informed judgement as 'academic' – whatever that might mean – or motivated by professional self-interest.[8] The evidence was all to the contrary. As Titmuss's comparative international study of the use of blood illustrated, the intrusion of commercial forces generated inefficiency and greater expense. In health policy there were no complex theoretical issues to reassess – no Robertson to oppose Keynes, as it were – and as a result nothing remotely like the revisionist debate over economic policy.

The new Conservative government responded with a marked lack of enthusiasm to the Black Report. It did not apply, however, the rhetoric about the morality and efficiency of market allocations to medical services with any real consistency. Ministers frequently stated they wanted to protect the NHS against financial pressure, and their insistence that it was safe in their hands apparently singled it out as an area where continuity was the aim. Nevertheless, since 1911 policy had been based on broad agreement, outside and inside government circles, that had tended to limit pressure-group activity, to resolve conflicts of interest, to form public debate and to maintain a sense of progress. The changes after 1979 provoked controversy without fragmenting this consensus, which was not destroyed or even weakened so much as forced into opposition.

Family Allowances

Beveridge's third assumption, that children's or family allowances were an essential part of an adequate system of social security, was the most obvious and perhaps the only real victim of the White Paper's substitution of the principle of 'reasonable' for 'subsistence' maintenance. Though the calculations of his expert advisors may now seem dubious, their validity is scarcely an issue, since the new allowances were far less than the amount which Beveridge had recommended. He had wanted 8s. a week to be paid for every dependent child in the family except the first – a sum reached by calculating the cost of full subsistence as 7s. at prewar prices, updating it to 9s. in line with inflation, and then reducing it by 1s. to take account of free school meals and milk. In 1945 the introductory rate was 5s., which had been mentioned so often during the previous long campaign for family allowances that the force of convention perhaps supported it. Certainly nothing else did.

Beveridge's recommendation that the first child should not be covered perhaps had invited this scaling down of support. He had argued in justification that it was dangerous to weaken parental responsibility too much, and also that family income was normally sufficient to support one child. This second claim, whatever its truth, was beside the point, if the aim was to cover needs fully, and it may have reflected some self-delusion or wishful thinking on his part, since by omitting the first child, according to his own calculations, he was cutting the projected cost of his proposals by almost half. The effect was even more dramatic in the Treasury Memorandum of May 1942, which had surveyed the case for family allowances without reaching any firm conclusions. It had calculated that, if the first child was not covered, the annual cost of allowances of 5s. a week would fall from £132 million to £58 million. Beveridge, moreover, had admitted that once the principle of meeting subsistence needs fully had been breached, there were arguments for reducing expenditure further, by excluding the second child as well, or lowering the amount paid for the third child and subsequent children, since clothing could be passed on and similar savings made in their case. He had defined his objective as a sharing of maintenance between parents and the community, and the implication that family expenditure was being subsidized, rather than full maintenance provided, was reinforced by the change of language from 'children's allowances' in the 1942 Report to 'family allowances' in the 1945 Act.

Except on this issue, however, Beveridge was very influential in clearing away the doubts and uncertainties which the Treasury Memorandum had expressed or papered over. He argued that children's allowances had to be financed entirely from general taxation, for otherwise insurance contributions would be pushed unbearably high for those on low pay and become too great a burden on employment. He also argued that any reasonable means test would save very little money and made out a very clear case for a scheme which covered all families, whatever their income, at a time when civil servants in the Board of Education, the Treasury and other departments were still attracted to means-tested provisions in cash or kind as an alternative.

He left only one major question unanswered. The abolition of income tax rebates for children had previously been identified, especially by Keynes in 1940 in his pamphlet, *How to Pay for the War*, as a means of financing what was always going to be an expensive innovation, no matter how much its cost was trimmed by compromises. This option, however, quickly became less attractive, as income tax became heavier and wage rises brought most manual workers within its scope for the first time. Beveridge was concerned to safeguard the incentive to work, by keeping as wide a gap as possible between a family's income when its head was in employment and when he was not, and in the light of this concern it made no sense to blunt the impact of introduction of family allowances by ending child tax rebates. The leaders of the Family Endowment Society, the main pressure group, were also divided on the issue. Eleanor Rathbone wanted to keep tax rebates because she imagined that they encouraged a higher birth rate, while Eva Hubback wanted to abolish them on the grounds that they unfairly favoured the better-off. Their value had been cut from £60 to £50 in 1941, but subsequent budgets left them untouched, and despite inflation they were still substantially mitigating the effects of heavier taxation. In these circumstances there was no move to abolish them in order to recoup some of the cost of family allowances.

The Bill in general was widely welcomed, and its only two controversial features had nothing at all to do with the issues which had previously been seen as central. Initially it proposed that family allowances should be paid to the father, and only a passionate protest by Eleanor Rathbone, followed by a free vote in the Commons, reversed this clause in favour of payment to the mother. Since the end of the First World War she had placed their introduction at the centre of a programme of welfare feminism, and in supporting her most MPs apparently were influenced by sentiment. The original Bill also gave the government the power to exclude families covered by other arrangements, obviously aimed at servicemen, whose pay contained separation allowances for children. These had been introduced during the First World War and during the Second had the same role of supporting the dependants of men serving in the armed forces. They had recently been raised to 12s. 6d. a week for each child, but it was arguable that any apparent generosity was illusory, and that their real function was to keep down service pay. On this issue the government conceded of its own accord and announced that servicemen's families would not be disqualified. There were still complaints that the first child was not covered, that 5s. was not enough, and that it was not index-linking. On this and later occasions, however, such criticism never became very vocal, even in 1946 when the new national insurance scheme added 7s. 6d. for the first child to a married couple's benefit. Eleanor Rathbone seemed to speak for most people when she described the 1945 Act as the triumph of a great principle.

The obvious problem is to explain why the triumph was so long delayed, since the case for family allowances had been stated more or less fully for at least 20 years. The reluctance of prewar governments to commit themselves to new expenditure in an uncertain economic climate is not a sufficient explanation on its own. Family allowance schemes in other countries varied widely in cost and were financed in different ways, and it was conventional to argue, even if it was by no means a matter of agreement, that by moderating wage claims in one form or another they had a role to play in economic recovery. As John MacNicol has shown, the movement for their introduction in Britain was weakened not only by financial considerations but also paradoxically by the breadth of its appeal and the diversity of its support, and he considerably qualifies the emphasis on its inevitable progress in Mary Stock's biography of Eleanor Rathbone. In particular he suggests that the 1945 Act was a result of wartime changes more than the accumulated pressure of a long campaign.[9]

The case for family allowances could be presented in demographic terms by arguing that they would contribute to a higher birth rate, which in the 1930s seemed desirable on economic and military grounds; and this case could be given a eugenic twist, because larger families tended to be found at the bottom of the social scale, by arguing that especially middle-class parents of greater intelligence would be encouraged to have more children. Family allowances were usually presented, however, as an answer to the problem of low pay that was more effective and cheaper than the alternative of a statutory minimum wage. All the interwar social surveys revealed large numbers of children living below subsistence because of the inadequacy of their father's earnings; and Seebohm Rowntree was the best-known advocate of imposing on employers an obligation to pay all male workers a wage sufficient at least for the 'human needs' of a couple with three dependent children. However, in *The Disinherited Family*, which became the Bible of the movement for family allowances after its publication in 1924, Eleanor Rathbone dismissed this idea. She pointed out that a minimum wage set at Rowntree's level would leave untouched poverty among families of more than three children, and she bitterly attacked the waste of paying it to single men and married ones with no children or only one or two. Her criticism neglected the stringency of the definition of 'human needs', but was undoubtedly damaging in rejecting a statutory minimum wage on grounds other than industry's inability to afford it, which was the usual argument against it.

What had been achieved by 1939 was not at all clear. The propaganda of the Family Endowment Society could always be tailored to fit different audiences and occasions, any strong commitment to a particular scheme had been consistently avoided and matters of detail tended to be left in obscurity as potentially divisive. In a sense this was the problem, since a broad coalition of support had been created, which was weak, because it had so little in common. Even Rowntree was a convert of a kind, when in response to Rathbone's criticism he came out in favour of family allowances starting with the birth of a fourth child. Moreover, campaigning even of this protean quality could still be counter-productive in raising very sensitive issues. The association with eugenics became more controversial as the 1930s drew to a close but on the whole was probably a source of strength rather than weakness, especially as the Eugenics Society under the influence of Titmuss and others became more intellectually coherent and managed to dissociate itself from racism. Civil servants at the Ministry of Health and the Board of Education, however, were antagonized by claims that many children were malnourished, and developed a defensive hostility to the lobbying of the Family Endowment Society, the Children's Minimum Council and other groups. The Labour party and the TUC, after some initial hesitation, also became unsympathetic. They tended with some justification to see family allowances as a covert means of keeping down wages and only abandoned their suspicions after the formation of a National Government in 1940 had given them a new confidence in their influence over policy.

Part of Eleanor Rathbone's desire to create a broad coalition of support was an instinct to head-hunt, and one of her most notable captures was Beveridge. On reading *The Disinherited Family* he was instantly converted and introduced family allowances into the pay scales of the staff at the London School of Economics, where he was Director. He also carefully marshalled the Family Endowment Society's evidence to the Royal Commission on the Coal Industry, and its Report in 1926 recommended additions to a miner's pay for each child in his family as a means of softening the impact of the wage cuts which appeared to be the only means of restoring the industry's profitability. By the later 1930s, however, as Chairman of the Unemployment Insurance Statutory Committee Beveridge was resisting pressure from the TUC and the Children's Minimum Council (largely the leaders of the Family Endowment Society under another name) to advise the Minister of Labour to increase the dependants' allowances which were attached to unemployment benefit; and these were only raised (to 4s. for the first two children and 3s. for others in the family) after the outbreak of the war. The main priority as the Committee defined it, not always with complete openness and honesty, was to keep the amount of his benefit below what a claimant could reasonably expect to earn. In effect a 'wage stop', which formally restricted unemployment assistance in this way, was operating informally in national insurance, and evidence that the families of many claimants were living in unsatisfactory circumstances was being set aside.

In 1942 Beveridge's proposals for a universal scheme of children's allowances allowed an escape from this dilemma which had faced the Statutory Committee. Even as scaled down by the 1945 Act, they still significantly added to the family income of lower-paid workers, keeping it above both the poverty line and benefit level, and so protecting living standards without endangering the incentive to work. Beveridge was consistent in his concern to safeguard the labour market, and his assumptions and fears were widely shared. In 1944 in *Full Employment in a Free Society* he suggested that the conditions for the payment of insurance benefit might justifiably be stiffened in conditions of full employment; and James Meade felt that on an essential point he was to be congratulated for speaking with greater frankness than the government's *Employment Policy* White Paper. In official circles few doubted that a combination of family allowances, high benefits and full employment would weaken individual efforts to hold jobs and to search for new ones or, to make the same point in another way, that frictional unemployment would increase.

Nevertheless, by this time opinion had been transformed by the war. Fears that inflation was a consequence of full employment revived the idea that family allowances could prevent excessive wage settlements, and though the Treasury urged delay on the grounds that their introduction would itself be inflationary, this was an argument about the short rather than the long term. The demand for them also became caught up in the growing hopes and expectations of postwar improvements, the Labour party and the TUC endorsed it, and in 1942 Beveridge already saw his Committee's task as simply to settle the details of a scheme.

However, if the 1945 Act was a triumph, it was an extremely short-lived one. General wage rises first blunted the significance of the compromise on cost and then over the next 20 years produced a state of neglect which saw the face value of family allowances increase only twice. For a generation Beveridge's assumption A, child allowances, scarcely seemed necessary, given assumption C, maintenance of employment. By 1958 the scheme had fallen into such disregard that the responsible minister, Boyd-Carpenter – who as Minister of Pensions was outside the Cabinet – discovered to his surprise that the Treasury without consulting him was proposing to abolish family allowances for second children as part of a programme of spending cuts. In the event Thorneycroft, the Chancellor of the Exchequer, and his junior ministers, Powell and Birch, resigned when a deflationary course of action was rejected by the majority of the Cabinet, and the Radcliffe Committee on the Working of the Monetary System quickly reasserted Keynesian orthodoxy. This only meant, however, that the scheme was not pruned back but simply allowed to continue to wither as average wages continued to keep well ahead of inflation.

Family allowances were restored to the centre of political attention by the rediscovery of poverty, and the scheme's reform, through raising their value and extending them to the first child, became a major aim of the so-called 'poverty lobby' of new pressure groups, which emerged in the 1960s. Initial expectations of swift progress, however, were disappointed, and by 1969 the Child Poverty Action Group had realized that it had been wrong in believing, when it had formed four years earlier to campaign on essentially a single issue, that success would be easily achieved. Its case for reconstituting allowances, like Eleanor Rathbone's for their introduction, emphasized that child poverty was a consequence of low pay. However, the problem was no longer to the same extent one of large families, whose living standards were dragged down because wages adequate to support one or two children could not stretch further. From surveys it appeared that in about a third of households with low income, where the head was in employment, there only was a single dependent child; and it was this finding that made the extension of family allowances seem essential. The other new element in the CPAG propaganda was its combination of universalism and selectivity. Its aim was not only to increase family allowances substantially in real terms but also to abolish income tax relief for children in order to claw back much of the cost from parents with higher incomes. In this way full take-up and easy administration, the characteristics of universalism, would be combined with targetting children in real need, and the overall cost to the Exchequer contained within reasonable limits.

Between 1964 and 1970 Labour governments found themselves under constant economic pressure. The new Cabinet inherited huge balance of payments deficits, which forced it first to abandon its National Plan and then to devalue sterling; and the period in office ended with an incomes freeze and deflation in an effort to make the devaluation of November 1967 effective. When the party won the election in 1964, family allowances in real terms had fallen well below their

1945 level. No increase came, however, until 1968. Then they were more than doubled, and adjustments in tax allowances left standard income tax payers virtually in the same position as before. Since low wage-earners gained, the changes can be seen as a significant achievement of redistribution without means-testing.[10] They came nowhere near realizing the CPAG programme, however, and during Labour's last months in power the increase was being eroded by rising inflation. As a result family allowances became an election issue in 1970, with the CPAG alleging that poverty had increased under Labour, and the Conservatives, apparently influenced by this argument, promising to finance another substantial increase through further tax adjustments.

Afterwards, in a sudden reversal of policy, the new Conservative government announced that it would introduce new means-tested payments instead, and as family income support these quickly came into force in 1971. At the time the explanation seemed a personal one – the death of Ian Macleod just after he had become Chancellor of the Exchequer and the replacement of his influence by Keith Joseph's. The origins of family income support, however, went back to preparations for means-tested family allowances by the Department of Health and Social Security in 1967, which Labour ministers had decided not to implement. By 1970 this option had become more attractive, because, as the new Cabinet apparently belatedly realized, the income tax threshold had fallen so low that child tax allowances had become important for maintaining the living standards of many poorer families. Certainly Conservative ministers appeared just as reluctant as their Labour predecessors to risk unpopularity by ending tax relief, and an intellectually respectable case could be made out for its social value. Frank Field, who became Director of the CPAG in 1969, claimed that Margaret Wynn's analysis of the effects of fiscal and welfare measures on family income supported its programme, and perhaps to some extent it did. She had actually demonstrated, however, that tax relief was important in reducing the heavy burdens of child rearing for the majority of families within a broad range of incomes.[11]

Whatever the precise reasons for its introduction, family income support quickly proved to be far from a final solution. Its low take-up in fact immediately demonstrated in an extreme form the defects of selectivity. Between 1971 and 1974 only about 48 per cent of those eligible applied for it, and even towards the end of the decade it was reaching only slightly over half the families for whom it was intended. In these circumstances Conservatives quickly became disillusioned with their creation and during the two elections in 1974 in various statements described it as a purely temporary measure, which would be superseded by other arrangements. Like Labour a decade earlier, the party appeared to be flirting with the idea of negative income tax assessments, and its leaders certainly accepted that any alternative had to reach families on low incomes comprehensively.

In the event Labour's narrow victories left it to implement the policies which it had avoided accepting completely during its last spell in government. The 1978 Child Benefit Act phased out child tax relief over three years and replaced family allowances by child benefit, which covered all dependent children. The financial impact was substantial, and in 1980-1, as tax allowances finally ended, child benefits were costing more than supplementary benefits. Like the failure to introduce family allowances before 1945, however, the lost decade from 1968 to 1978 cannot simply be put down to the climate of economic uncertainty. The economy was, if anything, in worse difficulty, and the immediate concern of Labour ministers seems always to have been the level of taxation rather than the state of the economy. According to Joel Barnett, whose memoirs give one of the frankest inside accounts of the 1974 Labour governments, Callaghan and Healey until the very end were extremely reluctant to reduce take-home pay by abolishing child tax allowances and, before accepting the compromise which phased them out, insisted on the TUC's agreement.[12] The history of the changes, partly because of the 30-year rule, tends to be written as a study of pressure-group activity, but like the Family Endowment Society earlier the Child Poverty Action Group was often ineffective. Field credits its campaigns and lobbying with having changed the attitudes of politicians, but the weight of evidence suggests that at most its influence was marginal.

The poverty lobby's limitations were shown not only by Labour ministers' reluctance to grasp the nettle until 1978 but also by the subsequent failure of child benefit to retain its value. After 1978, as increases lagged behind inflation, it quickly began to suffer the same fate as family allowances. Even at the very beginning the introductory rate was not high enough for family income support to be abolished, and if this had happened, most families on it would have been worse off despite the new child benefits. In fact, far from contracting, the scope of family income support expanded. The Finer Committee saw it as an answer to some of the needs of one-parent families, which were attracting increasing attention, and in 1979 the minimum number of working hours required to qualify was reduced to allow more single parents to apply. In 1982, when the Conservative government updated it, unlike other benefits it kept its value in real terms. By this time the number of families receiving it had virtually doubled since 1979 (from around 78,000 to 140,000), and the cost of abolishing it by raising child benefits sufficiently was estimated to be about £8 billion. Its retention was never in any doubt, and all that changed was its name in 1988 to family credit.

The introduction of family allowances was the only assumption set out in detail in the Beveridge Report. They were intimately related to the Plan's basic aim of maintaining income: along with sickness and unemployment benefits and retirement pensions, a fourth form of support which was universally available, and the only difference was that they were not financed partly from insurance contributions. Their history like that of national insurance can be resolved without oversimplification into an attempt to shore up universalism. In both cases by 1988 this had largely failed or been abandoned, though the extent of failure and the reasons for it may remain open to some debate.

Notes

1 'Sir William Beveridge's *Full Employment in a Free Society* and the White Paper on Employment Policy (Cmnd 6527)', in Susan Howson (ed.), *The Collected Papers of James Meade* (1988) Vol. I, pp. 233-64.
2 The article, originally published in the *Economic Journal*, is reprinted in Charles Feinstein (ed.), *The Managed Economy: Essays on British Economic Policy and Performance since 1929* (1983).
3 Nicholas Kaldor, *The Scourge of Monetarism* (1982).
4 *Social Insurance and Allied Services*, p. 120.
5 Rudolf Klein, *The Politics of the National Health Service* (1983).
6 Brian Watkin, *The National Health Service: The First Phase, 1948-1974 and After* (1978).
7 *Inequalities in Health: The Black Report; The Health Divide*, (1988), p. 43.
8 David G. Green, *Working-class Patients and the Medical Establishment: Self-help in Britain from the Mid- nineteenth Century to 1948* (1985) (especially the remarks on pp. 3-5 about 'prevailing academic theories' and the 'dominant academic view').
9 John MacNicol, *The Movement for Family Allowances* (1981).
10 Wilfrid Beckermann (ed.), *The Labour Government's Economic Record, 1964-70* (1972).
11 Margaret Wynn, *Family Policy* (1970); Frank Field, *Poverty and Politics: The Inside Story of the CPAG Campaigns in the 1970s* (1982).
12 Joel Barnett, *Inside the Treasury* (1982).

4

Progress and Decline

By the late 1970s there was a growing acceptance that the Welfare State was in decline. The contraction of national insurance and the widening scope of means-tested benefits clearly indicated that Beveridge's universalism was under considerable strain, and failures of economic management had brought into question the ability of any government to secure the stable growth in the economy that seemed necessary to fund adequate health and social services and to prevent them from coming under potentially crippling pressure. It was not a paradox that in real terms most benefits were higher than ever, since the total bill contributed to the perception that the whole welfare system was creaking under pressure, and there could be no doubting that relative poverty, however it was defined, was extensive.

Subsequently this decline apparently became more marked, as Conservative governments after 1979 repudiated much of the previous orthodoxy, which had been formed by Beveridge and Keynes, occasionally with regret that it had become outdated, but more often explicitly and positively by substituting a new political rhetoric or ideology. Some of the policies of the 1980s, such as the privatization of public utilities or the reduction of local government responsibilities, seem an attack on the Victorian administrative State rather than on the Welfare State as it had been conventionally seen, and a degree of continuity with the past was preserved, if for no other cause than the persistence of a gap between the intentions and effects of government actions. The level of public expenditure on welfare remained substantially unchanged. The Fowler review placed the main responsibility for meeting needs squarely on means-tested benefits, but for years the numbers of families and individuals receiving them had been increasing despite the aim of successive governments not to allow this to happen. However, a cluster of related policies and social objectives were either abandoned completely or assigned a much lower priority: progressive and redistributive taxation; the attempt to define and to maintain a reasonable minimum standard of living below which no one would fall; the effort to find the right balance between the effectiveness of universally available benefits and services and the relative cheapness of means-tested ones; the willingness not to impose arbitrary budgetary ceilings; and perhaps too deference to the conclusions of informed opinion and debate, though both of these were losing at least some of their former coherence. If not always very clearly, both the content and spirit of social legislation was changing.

Nevertheless, the concept of decline is elusive, and the tendency to identify the 20 years or so after the Second World War as the classic phase of the Welfare State in Britain is highly ambiguous. What made this period so distinctive was full employment. During it the assumption was abandoned that poverty had virtually disappeared, and piecemeal reforms added to or modified the immediate postwar legislation, which had largely implemented the Beveridge Plan, in an effort to make its operation more effective. The result, however, could hardly be described as success. By 1972, while James Meade accepted that 'so many intangible social, psychological and moral issues' were involved that 'a fundamental definition of poverty' was impossible, he had no doubt at all that impoverishment existed on an extensive scale and that 'The relief of poverty is in a terrible muddle in this country.'[1] The confidence and optimism of the consensus on economic and social policy, which he had helped to form, had dissolved long before Thatcherite Conservatism gained power in 1979.

Perhaps it is possible to dispense to some extent at least with the notion of progress and decline. Shifting constraints on policy have been imposed by long-term economic and demographic trends, by the development of private insurance, by the accommodation of different professional and sectional interests, and by changes in conventional values and in economic theory, and all these factors have prevented its goals from being securely fixed. Nevertheless, Beveridge's belief in 1942 that substantial improvements in social security and medical care had been made since the start of the century was true, and the acceptance of his recommendations and assumptions produced further improvements. His vision of a society combining freedom of choice with secure minimum living standards, high enough for surviving inequalities to become insignificant, could scarcely at any time be called outdated, and the rhetoric of the morality of markets and the inefficiency of intervention and regulation in practice produced at least as wide a gap between the claims which were made for policies and their actual results.

Access to Cabinet and departmental papers under the 30-year rule has removed whatever undue emphasis on progress there may previously have been and given a greater insight into the compromises made by governments to build up support or to reconcile divergent interests. Despite failures of analysis or intention, however, policy was influenced by informed debate, to which political lobbying and pressure groups of different kinds contributed. Their activity, of course, had other aspects, but it also contributed intrinsically to the process of rational analysis and the formation of general agreement. The evidence on the whole supports the democratic pluralist view that separate interests far from being at odds with some concept of a national interest are essential for creating one.

Governments, of course, always had freedom to decide priorities and to choose among a variety of options, whatever the political and economic constraints on their actions. The Royal Commission on health insurance answered arguments from the approved societies that contractual obligations existed which could not be unilaterally abrogated, by describing the scheme in 1926 as a vast experiment upon which parliament had embarked, and which it could change as it liked. In the event the Conservative government did not limit the autonomy of the societies in the way the Majority of the Royal Commission recommended. However, at more or less the same time as it conceded to their pressure, it rejected the Blanesburgh Committee's proposed financial restructuring of unemployment insurance, which had the strong support of many Conservative businessmen and industrialists. Twenty years later, though Beveridge had wanted to retain it in a much modified form, indirect administration was abolished completely. Such examples could easily be multiplied to support Beveridge's belief in 1942 that progress was a matter of political will as well as the correct policies. The Welfare State's history can only finally be written as some sort of liberal narrative of progress, decline and potential recovery with the volume of poverty and the extent of redistribution the central issues.

Note

1 'Poverty in the Welfare State', in Susan Howson (ed.), *The Collected Papers of James Meade*, Vol. II (1988).

Bibliography

Abel-Smith, Brian, *The Hospitals, 1800–1948: A Study in Social Administration in England and Wales* (Heinemann, London, 1964).

Abel-Smith, Brian and Townsend, Peter, *The Poor and the Poorest* (Bell, London, 1965).

Addison, Paul, *The Road to 1945: British Politics and the Second World War* (Cape, London, 1975).

Addison, Paul, 'The Road to 1945', in Hennessy, P. and Seldon, Anthony (eds), *Ruling Performance: British Governments from Attlee to Thatcher* (Basil Blackwell, Oxford, 1987).

Adler, Michael and Bradley, Anthony (eds), *Justice, Discretion and Supplementary Benefit Tribunals in Britain* (Professional Books, London, 1976).

Alford, B. W. E., *Depression and Recovery: British Economic Growth, 1918–1939* (Macmillan, London, 1972).

Ashford, Douglas, *The Emergence of the Welfare States* (Basil Blackwell, Oxford, 1986).

Atkinson, A. B., *Poverty in Britain and the Reform of Social Security* (Cambridge University Press, Cambridge, 1970).

Atkinson, A. B., *The Economics of Inequality* (Clarendon Press, Oxford, 1975).

Atkinson, A. B., *Poverty and Social Security* (Harvester Wheatsheaf, Hemel Hempstead, 1989).

Bakke, A. W., *The Unemployed Man* (Nisbet, London, 1933).

Banting, K., *Poverty, Politics and Policy: Britain in the 1960s* (Macmillan, London, 1979).

Barnett, Corelli, *The Audit of War: The Illusion and Reality of Britain as a Great Nation* (Macmillan, London, 1986).

Barnett, Joel, *Inside the Treasury* (Deutsch, London, 1982).

Bartrip, Peter (ed.), *Workmen's Compensation in Twentieth Century Britain* (Gower, Aldershot, 1987).

Beckermann, W. (ed.), *The Labour Government's Economic Record, 1964–70* (Duckworth, London, 1972).

Beckermann, Wilfrid and Clark, Stephen, *Poverty and Social Security in Britain since 1961* (Oxford University Press, Oxford, 1982).

Benn, Tony, *Out of the Wilderness: Diaries, 1963–67* (Hutchinson, London, 1988).

Benn, Tony, *Office without Power: Diaries, 1968–72* (Hutchinson, London, 1988).

Bernstein, G. L., *Liberalism and Liberal Politics in Edwardian England*, (Allen & Unwin, London, 1986).

Berthoud, R. and Brown, J. C., with Cooper, S., *Poverty and the Development of Anti-Poverty Policies in the United Kingdom* (Heinemann, London, 1981).

Beveridge, Janet, *Beveridge and his Plan* (Hodder & Stoughton, London, 1954).

Beveridge, Sir William, *Insurance for All and Everything* (Daily News Ltd, London, 1924).

Beveridge, Sir William, *Unemployment, A Problem of Industry* (Longmans, London, 1930).

Beveridge, Sir William, *Full Employment in a Free Society* (Allen & Unwin, London, 1944).

Beveridge, Lord, *Voluntary Action* (Allen & Unwin, London, 1948).

Beveridge, Lord, *Power and Influence* (Hodder & Stoughton, London, 1953).

Bock, Gisela and Thane, Pat (eds), *Maternity and Gender Policies: Women and the Rise of European Welfare States, 1880s–1950s* (Routledge, London, 1991).

Booth, Alan, *British Economic Policy, 1931–49: Was there a Keynesian Revolution?* (Harvester Wheatsheaf, Hemel Hempstead, 1989).

Booth, Alan, 'Britain in the 1930s: A Managed Economy?', *Economic History Review*, XL, No. 4, 1987, pp. 499–556.

Booth, Alan, 'Britain in the 1930s: A Managed Economy? A Reply to Peden and Middleton', and Peden, G. C., 'A comment', and Middleton, Roger, 'A comment', *Economic History Review*, XLII, No. 4, 1989, pp. 548–56.

Booth, Alan and Pack, Melvyn, *Employment, Capital and Economic Policy, Great Britain, 1918–1939* (Basil Blackwell, Oxford, 1985).

Boyd-Carpenter, John, *Way of Life* (Sidgwick & Jackson, London, 1980).

Bransom, Nora, *Poplarism, 1919–1925* (Lawrence & Wishart, London, 1979).

Briggs, Asa, *Social Thought and Social Action: A Study of the Work of Seebohm Rowntree, 1971–1954* (Longmans, London, 1961).

Briggs, Asa, 'The Welfare State in Historical Perspective', *The Collected Essays*, II (Harvester, Brighton, 1985).

Briggs, E. and Rees, A. M., *Supplementary Benefits and the Consumer* (Bedford Square Press, London, 1980).

Brown, R. G. S., *The Management of Welfare: A Study of British Social Service Administration* (Martin Robertson, London, 1975).

Bryher, L., *Below the Magic Mountain: A Social History of Tuberculosis in Twentieth-Century Britain* (Clarendon Press, Oxford, 1988).

Bullock, Alan, *Life and Times of Ernest Bevin*, Vol. II, *Minister of Labour, 1940–45* (Heinemann, London, 1967).

Bulmer, Martin, Lewis, Jane and Piachaud, David, *The Goals of Social Policy* (Unwin Hyman, London, 1989).

Bunbury, Sir Henry N. (ed.), *Lloyd George's Ambulance Wagon, Being the Memoirs of William J. Braithwaite* (Methuen & Co., London, 1957).

Burk, Kathleen (ed.), *War and the State: The Transformation of British Government, 1914–1919* (Allen & Unwin, London, 1982).

Burk, Kathleen and Cairncross, Alex, *'Goodbye Great Britain': The 1976 IMF Crisis* (Yale University Press, New Haven and London, 1992).

Burnett, John, *Idle Hands: The Experience of Unemployment* (Routledge, London, 1994).

Cairncross, Alec, *Years of Recovery: British Economic Policy, 1945–51* (Methuen, London, 1985).

Cairncross, Alec, *Is There No Cure for Unemployment?* (Glasgow University, Glasgow, 1989).

Cairncross, Alec and Watts, Nita, *The Economic Section, 1939–1961* (Routledge, London, 1989).

Carpenter, G., 'National Health Insurance: A Case Study of the Use of Non-profit Making Organisations in the Provision of Welfare Benefits', *Public Administration*, 62, 1984, pp. 71–89.

Casson, Mark, *Economics and Unemployment, An Historical Perspective* (Martin Robertson, Oxford, 1983).

Castle, Barbara, *The Castle Diaries, 1974–76* (George Weidenfeld & Nicolson, London, 1980).

Castle, Barbara, *The Castle Diaries, 1964–70* (George Weidenfeld & Nicolson, London, 1984).

Clarke, Peter, 'The Politics of Keynesian Economics', in Bentley, M. and Stevenson, J. (eds), *High and Low Politics in Modern Britain* (Clarendon Press, Oxford, 1983).

Clarke, Peter, *The Keynesian Revolution in the Making, 1924–1936* (Clarendon Press, Oxford, 1988).

Cooper, M. H. (ed.), *Social Policy: A Survey of Recent Developments* (Basil Blackwell, Oxford, 1973).

Crossman, Richard, *Diaries of a Cabinet Minister, I* (Hamilton & Cape, London, 1975), *II* (1976), *III* (1977).

Crowther, Anne, *The Workhouse System, 1834–1939* (Batsford, London, 1981).

Crowther, Anne, *British Social Policy, 1914–1939* (Macmillan, London, 1988).

Cutler, Tony, Williams, Karel and Williams, John, *Keynes, Beveridge and Beyond* (Routledge & Kegan Paul, London, 1986).

Cypher, J. (ed.), *Seebohm Across Three Decades* (British Association of Social Workers, London, 1979).

Dahl, Robert A. and Lindblom, Charles E., *Politics, Economics and Welfare* (Chicago University Press, Chicago, 1976).

Dahl, Robert A., *Dilemmas of Pluralist Democracy* (Yale University Press, New Haven, 1982).

Davidson, Roger, *Whitehall and the Labour Problem in late Victorian and Edwardian Britain* (Croom Helm, London, 1985).

Davison, R. C., *The Unemployed and British Unemployment Policy* (Longmans, London, 1930)

Davison, R. C., *British Unemployment Policy: The Modern Phase since 1930* (Longmans, London, 1938).

Deacon, Alan, *In Search of the Scrounger: The Administration of Unemployment Insurance in Britain, 1920–31* (Bell, London, 1976).

Deacon, Alan, 'Coercion and Conciliation: The Politics of Unemployment in the 1920s', in Briggs, A. and Saville, J. (eds), *Essays in Labour History, II* (Croom Helm, London, 1977).

Deacon, Alan and Bradshaw, Jonathan, *Reserved for the Poor: The Means Test in British Social Policy* (Martin Robertson, Oxford, 1983).

Digby, Anne, *British Welfare Policy* (Faber & Faber, London, 1989).

Digby, Anne and Bosanquet, Nick, 'Doctors and Patients in the Era of National Health Insurance and Private Practice', *Economic History Review*, XLI, No. 1, 1988, pp. 74–94.

Dilnot, A. W., Kay, J. A. and Morris, C. N., *The Reform of Social Security* (Clarendon Press, Oxford, 1984).

Donnison, David, *The Politics of Poverty* (Martin Robertson, Oxford, 1982).

Donoghue, Bernard, *Prime Minister: The Conduct of Policy under Harold Wilson and James Callaghan* (Jonathan Cape, London, 1987).

Durbin, Elizabeth, *New Jerusalems: The Labour Party and the Economics of Democratic Socialism* (Routledge & Kegan Paul, London, 1985).

Dwork, Deborah, *War is Good for Babies and Other Young Children: A History of the Infant and Child Welfare Movement in England, 1898–1918* (Tavistock, London, 1987).

Eder, Norman, *National Health Insurance and the Medical Profession in Britain, 1913–39* (Garland Publishers, New York and London, 1982).

Ekstein, H., *The English Health Service* (Harvard University Press, Cambridge, 1958).

Feinstein, Charles (ed.), *The Managed Economy: Essays on British*

Economic Policy and Performance since 1929 (Oxford University Press, Oxford, 1983).

Field, Frank *Poverty and Politics: The Inside Story of the CPAG Campaigns in the 1970s* (Heinemann, London, 1982).

Fildes, Valerie, Marks, Lara and Marland, Hilary (eds), *Women and Children First: International Maternal and Infant Welfare* (Routledge, London, 1992).

Finlayson, Geoffrey, 'A Moving Frontier: Voluntaryism and the State in British Social Welfare, 1941–1949', 20th Century British History, 1, 2, 1990, pp. 183–206.

Finlayson, Geoffrey, *Citizen, State and Social Welfare in Britain, 1830–1990* (Clarendon Press, Oxford, 1994).

Floud, R. and McCloskey, D. N. (eds), *The Economic History of Britain since 1700, II* (Cambridge, University Press, Cambridge 1981).

Foot, Michael, *Aneurin Bevan, II, 1945–60* (Davis-Poynter, London, 1973).

Forsyth, Gordon, *Doctors and State Medicine: A Study of the British Health Service* (Pitman Medical, London, 1972).

Fraser, Derek, *Evolution of the Welfare State* (Macmillan, London, 1984).

Freeden, Michael, *The New Liberalism: An Ideology of Social Reform* (Clarendon Press, Oxford, 1978).

George, Victor, *Social Security: Beveridge and After* (Routledge & Kegan Paul, London, 1968).

George, Victor, *Social Security and Society* (Routledge & Kegan Paul, London, 1973).

George, Victor and Howard, Irving, *Poverty amidst Affluence: Britain and the United States* (Edward Elgar, Aldershot, 1991).

Gilbert, Bentley B., 'The Decay of Provident Institutions and the Coming of Old Age Pensions in Britain', *Economic History Review*, XVII, No. 3, 1965, pp. 551–63.

Gilbert, Bentley B., *The Evolution of National Insurance in Great Britain* (Michael Joseph, London, 1966).

Gilbert, Bentley B., *British Social Policy, 1918–39* (Batsford, London, 1970).

Gilbert, Bentley B., 'David Lloyd George, the Reform of British Landholding and the Budget of 1914', *Historical Journal*, 21, 1, 1978, pp. 117–41.

Gilbert, Bentley B., *David Lloyd George, A Political Life: The Architect of Change, 1863–1914* (Batsford, London, 1987).

Gilmour, Ian, *Dancing with Dogma: Britain under Thatcherism* (Simon & Schuster, London, 1992).

Glynn, Sean, *No Alternative? Unemployment in Britain* (Faber & Faber, London, 1991).

Glynn, Sean and Booth, Alan (eds), *The Road to Full Employment* (Allen & Unwin, London, 1987).

Goldman, Peter, *The Welfare State* (Michael Joseph, London, 1964).

Gosden, P. H. J. H., *Self-help: Voluntary Associations in the Nineteenth Century* (B. T. Batsford, London, 1973).

Gospel, H. F. and Littler, C. R. (eds), *Managerial Strategies and Industrial Relations: An Historical and Comparative Study* (Heinemann, London, 1983).

Gray, Alexander, *Some Aspects of National Health Insurance* (P. S. King and Son, London, 1923).

Green, David G., *Working-class Patients and the Medical Establishment* (Gower and Maurice Temple Smith, London, 1985).

Hall, Peter (ed.), *Labour's New Frontiers* (Deutsch, London, 1964).

Hall, Phoebe, *Reforming the Welfare* (Heinemann, London, 1976).

Hall, Phoebe, Land, Hilary, Parker, Roy and Webb, Adrian, *Change, Choice and Conflict* (Heinemann, London, 1975).

Hannah, Leslie, *Inventing Retirement: The Development of Occupational Pensions in Britain* (Cambridge University Press, Cambridge, 1986).

Harris, Jose, *Unemployment and Politics: A Study in English Social Policy, 1886-1914* (Clarendon Press, Oxford, 1972).

Harris, Jose, *William Beveridge* (Clarendon Press, Oxford, 1977).

Harris, Jose, 'Did British Workers Want the Welfare State? G. D. C. Cole's Survey of 1942', in Winter, J. (ed.), *The Working Class in Modern Britain* (Cambridge University Press, Cambridge, 1983).

Harris, Jose, 'Social Planning in Wartime', in Winter, J. (ed.), *War and Economic Development* (Cambridge University Press, Cambridge, 1975).

Harris, Jose, 'Enterprise and Welfare States: A Comparative Perspective', *Transactions of the Royal Historical Society*, 40, 1990, pp. 175-95.

Harris, Jose, 'Political Thought and the Welfare State, 1940-1970: An Intellectual Framework for British Social Policy', *Past and Present*, 135, 1992, pp. 161-208.

Harrod, Sir Roy, *Life of John Maynard Keynes* (Macmillan, London, 1951).

Hay, Denys, 'British Historians and the Beginnings of the Civil History of the Second World War', in Foot, M. R. D. (ed.), *War and Society* (Elek, London, 1973).

Hay, J. R., 'Employers and Social Policy in Britain: The Evolution of Welfare Legislation, 1905-14', *Social History*, 2, 1977, pp. 435-55.

Hay, J. R., *The Origins of British Welfare Reforms* (Macmillan, London, 1978).

Hemming, Richard, *Poverty and Incentives: The Economics of Social Security* (Oxford University Press, Oxford, 1984).

Hendrick, Harry, *Child Welfare: England 1872-1989* (Routledge, London, 1994).

Hennessy, Peter, *Never Again: Britain 1945-51* (Cape, London, 1992).

Hennock, E. P., *British Social Reform and German Precedents: The Case of Social Insurance* (Clarendon Press, Oxford, 1987).

Hicks, John, *The Crisis of Keynesian Economics* (Basil Blackwell, Oxford, 1974).

Hill, Michael, *Social Security Policy in Great Britain* (Edward Elgar, Aldershot, 1990).

Hills, John (ed.), *The State of Welfare: The Welfare State in Britain since 1974* (Clarendon Press, Oxford, 1990).

Honigsbaum, Frank, *The Division in British Medicine: The History of the Separation of General Practitioners from Hospital Care, 1911–1948* (Kogan Page, London, 1979).

Honigsbaum, Frank, *Health, Happiness and Security* (Routledge, London, 1989).

Howson, Susan (ed.), *The Collected Papers of James Meade, I* and *II* (Allen & Unwin, London, 1988).

Howson, Susan and Winch, Donald, *The Economic Advisory Council, 1930–39* (Cambridge University Press, Cambridge, 1977).

Hutchison, T. W., *Keynes versus the 'Keynsians'* (Institute for Economic Affairs, London, 1977).

Hutchison, T. W., *On Revolutions and Progress in Economic Knowledge* (Cambridge University Press, Cambridge, 1978).

Inequalities in Health: The Black Report; The Health Divide (Penguin Press, Harmondsworth, 1988).

Johnson, Norman, *Reconstructing the Welfare State* (Harvester Wheatsheaf, London, 1990).

Johnson, Paul B., *Land Fit for Heroes* (University of Chicago Press, Chicago and London, 1968).

Jones, Russell, *Wages and Employment Policy, 1936–1985* (Allen & Unwin, London, 1987).

Kaldor, Nicholas, *The Scourge of Monetarism* (Oxford University Press, Oxford, 1982).

Kay, J. A. and King, M. A., *The British Tax System* (Oxford University Press, Oxford, 1983).

Kincaid, J. C., *Poverty and Equality in Britain* (Penguin Press, Harmondsworth, 1973).

Klein, Rudolf, *Complaints against Doctors* (C. Knight, London, 1973).

Klein, Rudolf, *The Politics of the National Health Service* (Longman, London, 1983).

Land, Hilary, 'The Family Wage,' *Feminist Review*, 6, 1980, pp. 55–77.

Levitt, Ian, 'The Scottish Poor Law and Unemployment', in Smout, T. C. (ed.), *The Search for Wealth and Stability* (Macmillan, London, 1979).

Levitt, Ian, *Poverty and Welfare in Scotland, 1890–1948* (Edinburgh University Press, Edinburgh, 1988).

Levitt, Ruth and Wall, Andrew, *The Reorganisation of the National Health Service* (Chapman & Hall, London, 1984).

Lewis, Jane, *The Politics of Motherhood: Child and Maternal Welfare in England, 1898–1918* (Croom Helm, London, 1980).

Lewis, Jane (ed.), *Women's Welfare, Women's Rights* (Croom Helm, London, 1983).

Lowe, Rodney, 'The Failure of Consensus in Britain: The National Industrial Conference', *Historical Journal*, 21, 3, 1978, pp. 649–75.

Lowe, Rodney, 'The Erosion of State Intervention in Britain, 1917–24', *Economic History Review*, XXXI, 2, 1978, pp. 270–86.

Lowe Rodney, 'Welfare Legislation and Unions During and After the First World War', *Historical Journal*, 25, 2, 1982, pp. 431–41.

Lowe, Rodney, 'Corporate bias, fact and fiction', in *Social Science Research Council Newsletter* (1983).

Lowe, Rodney, *Adjusting to Democracy: The Role of the Ministry of Labour in British Politics, 1916–1939* (Clarendon Press, Oxford, 1986).

Lowe, Rodney, 'Resignation at the Treasury: The Social Services Committee and the Failure to Reform the Welfare State', *Journal of Social Policy*, 18, 4, 1989, pp. 505–26.

Lowe, Rodney, 'The Second World War, Consensus and the Foundation of the Welfare State', 20th Century British History, 1, 2, 1990, pp. 152–82.

Lynes, Tony, *National Assistance and National Prosperity* (Codicote Press, Welwyn, 1962).

McBriar, A. M., *An Edwardian Mixed Doubles: The Bosanquets versus the Webbs* (Clarendon Press, Oxford, 1987).

McCarthy, Michael, *Campaigning for the Poor: The Child Poverty Action Group and the Politics of Welfare* (Croom Helm, London, 1986).

MacGregor, *The Politics of Poverty* (Longman, London, 1981).

Mackenzie, W. J. M., *Power and Responsibility in Health Care: The National Health Service as a Political Institution* (Oxford University Press, Oxford, 1979).

McLaine, Ian, *Ministry of Morale: Home Front Morale and the Ministry of Information in World War II* (Allen & Unwin, London, 1979).

MacNalty, Sir Arthur S., *The Civil Health and Medical Services, I, History of the Second World War, United Kingdom Medical Series* (HMSO, London, 1953).

MacNicol, John, *The Movement for Family Allowances* (Heinemann, London, 1981).

Mair, Philip B., *Shared Enthusiasm: The Story of Lord and Lady Beveridge* (Ascent, Windlesham, 1982).

Marsh, David, *The Welfare State* (Londman, London, 1970).

Marshall, T. H., *Sociology at the Crossroads* (Heinemann, London, 1963).

Marshall, T. H., *Social Policy* (Hutchinson, London, 1975).

Marshall, T. H., *The Right to Welfare* (Heinemann, London, 1981).

Marwick, Arthur, 'Middle Opinion in the 'Thirties: Planning, Progress and Political Agreement', *English Historical Review*, LXXIX, 1964, pp. 285–98.

Marwick, Arthur, 'The Labour Party and the Welfare State in Britain', *American Historical Review*, 73, 1967–8, pp. 380–403.

Matthews, R. C. O., 'Why has Britain had Full Employment since the War?'

in Feinstein, Charles (ed.), *The Managed Economy: Essays on Economic Policy and Performance* (Oxford University Press, Oxford, 1983).

Middlemas, Keith, *Politics in Industrial Society: The Experience of the British System since 1911* (Deutsch, London, 1979).

Middlemas, Keith, 'Corporate Bias, a Response', in *Social Science Research Council Newsletter* (1983).

Middlemas, Keith, *Power, Competition and the State, I: Britain in Search of Balance* (Macmillan, London, 1986).

Middleton, Roger, *Towards the Managed Economy* (Methuen, London, 1985).

Miller, F. M., 'National Assistance and Unemployment Assistance – The British Cabinet and Relief Policy, 1932–3', *Journal of Contemporary History*, 9, 2, 1974, pp. 163–83.

Miller, F. M., 'The Unemployment Policy of the National Government, 1931–36', *Historical Journal*, XIX, 1976, pp. 453–76.

Miller, F. M., 'The British Unemployment Crisis of 1935', *Journal of Contemporary History*, 14, 2, 1979, pp. 329–51.

Millet, J. D., *The Unemployment Assistance Board* (Allen & Unwin, London, 1939).

Mommsen, W. J. (ed.), *The Emergence of the Welfare State in Britain and Germany* (Croom Helm, London, 1981).

Morgan, Janet (ed.), *The Backbench Diaries of Richard Crossman* (Hamilton & Cape, London, 1981).

Morgan, K. O., *Consensus and Disunity: The Lloyd George Coalition* (Clarendon Press, Oxford, 1979).

Mowat, C. L., *The Charity Organisation Society, 1869–1913* (Methuen, London, 1961).

Murray, Bruce K., *The People's Budget, 1909–10* (Clarendon Press, Oxford, 1980).

Myrdal, Gunnar, *Beyond the Welfare State* (Gerald Duckworth, London, 1960).

Parker, Julia, *Local Health and Welfare Services* (Allen & Unwin, London, 1965).

Parker, Julia, *Social Policy and Citizenship* (Macmillan, London, 1975).

Parry, N., Rustin, R. and Satyamurti, C. (eds), *Social Work, Welfare and the State* (Edward Arnold, London, 1979).

Pater, John E., *The Making of the National Health Service* (King Edward's Hospital Fund, London, 1981).

Patinkin, D. and Clark, J. (eds), *Keynes, Cambridge and the General Theory* (Macmillan, London, 1977).

Peacock, Alan T. and Wiseman, Jack, *The Growth of Public Expenditure in the United Kingdom* (George Allen & Unwin, London, 1967).

Peden, G. C., 'Sir Richard Hopkins and the "Keynesian Revolution in Economic Theory"', *Economic History Review*, XXVI, 2, 1983, pp. 281–96.

Peden, G. C., *British Economic and Social Policy, Lloyd George to Margaret Thatcher* (Philip Allan, Oxford, 1985).

Peden, G. C., *Keynes, the Treasury and British Economic Policy* (Macmillan, London, 1988).

Pederson, Susan, *Family, Dependence and the Origins of the Welfare State, Britain and France 1914-1945* (Cambridge University Press, Cambridge, 1993).

Pelling, Henry, *Popular Politics and Society in late Victorian Britain* (Macmillan, London, 1968).

Pelling, Margaret and Smith, Richard M. (eds), *Life, Death and the Elderly* (Routledge, London, 1991).

Phillips, Gordon and Whiteside, Noelle, *Casual Labour: The Unemployment Question in the Port Transport Industry, 1880-1970* (Clarendon Press, Oxford, 1985).

Phillips, Gordon, 'Trade Unions and Corporatist Politics: The Response of the T.U.C. to Rationalisation', in Waller, P. J. (ed.), *Politics and Social Change in Modern Britain* (Harvester, Brighton, 1977).

Pilgrim Trust, *Men without Work: A Report made to the Pilgrim Trust* (Cambridge, 1938).

Pimlott, Ben, *Hugh Dalton* (Cape, London, 1985).

Pimlott, Ben, *The Political Diary of Hugh Dalton* (Cape, London, 1986).

Pimlott, Ben, *Harold Wilson* (HarperCollins, London, 1992).

Pinder, J. (ed.), *Fifty Years of Social and Economic Planning* (Heinemann, London, 1981).

Political and Economic Planning, *Report on the British Social Services* (London, 1937).

Political and Economic Planning, *Report on the British Health Services* (London, 1937).

Reismann, W., *Richard Titmuss, Welfare and Society* (Heinemann, London, 1977).

Robbins, Lord, *The Autobiography of an Economist* (Macmillan, London, 1971).

Robson, W. A. (ed.), *Social Security* (George Allen & Unwin, London, 1944).

Rodgers, Terence, 'Employers' Organisations, Unemployment and Social Politics in Britain in the Interwar Period', *Social History*, 13, 1988, pp. 315-41.

Rollings, Neil, 'British Budgetary Policy, 1945-54: A "Keynesian Revolution"?' *Economic History Review*, XLI, 2, 1988, pp. 283-98.

Rooff, Madeleine, *A Hundred Years of Family Welfare* (Michael Joseph, London, 1972).

Rose, Michael, *The Relief of Poverty, 1834-1914* (Macmillan, London, 1974).

Ross, J. S., *The National Health Service in Great Britain: An Historical and Descriptive Study* (Oxford University Press, Oxford, 1952).

Rowntree, B. S. and Lavers, G. R., *Poverty and the Welfare State* (Longman, Green & Co., London, 1950).

Searle, G. R., *The Liberal Party, 1886–1929* (Macmillan, London, 1992).

Showler, Brian and Sinfield, Adrian (eds), *The Workless State* (Martin Robertson, London, 1981).

Skidelsky, Robert, *Politicians and the Slump* (Macmillan, London, 1967).

Skidelsky, Robert (ed.), *The End of the Keynesian Era* (Macmillan, London, 1977).

Sleeman, J. F., *The Welfare State, Its Aims, Benefits and Costs* (George Allen & Unwin, London, 1973).

Smith, F. B., *The Retreat of Tuberculosis, 1850–1950* (Croom Helm, London, 1988).

Smith, Harold L. (ed.), *War and Social Change: British Society in the Second World War* (Manchester University Press, Manchester, 1986).

Stevenson, Olive, *Claimant or Client?* (George Allen & Unwin, London, 1973).

Stocks, Mary, *Eleanor Rathbone* (Gollanz, London, 1949).

Thane, Pat (ed.), *Origins of Modern Social Policy* (Croom Helm, London, 1978).

Thane, Pat, *The Foundations of the Welfare State* (Longman, London, 1982).

Thane, Pat, 'The Working Class and State "Welfare" in Britain', *Historical Journal*, 27, 4, 1984, pp. 877–900.

Thane, Pat, 'The British Welfare State: Its Origins and Character', in Digby, Anne and Feinstein, Charles (eds), *New Directions in Social and Economic History* (MacMillan, London, 1989).

Timms, Noel, *Pyschiatric Social Work in Great Britain* (Routledge & Kegan Paul, London, 1964).

Titmuss, R. M., *Problems of Social Policy* (HMSO, London, 1950).

Titmuss, R. M., *Essays on 'The Welfare State'* (George Allen & Unwin, London, 1958; 2nd edn, 1963).

Titmuss, R. M., *Income Distribution and Social Change* (George Allen & Unwin, London, 1962).

Titmuss, R. M., *Commitment to Welfare* (George Allen & Unwin, London, 1968).

Titmuss., R. M., *The Gift Relationship* (George Allen & Unwin, London, 1970).

Titmuss, R. M., *Social Policy* (George Allen & Unwin, London, 1974).

Tomlinson, J., *Monetarism: Is There An Alternative?* (Basil Blackwell, Oxford, 1986).

Tomlinson, J., *Employment Policy: The Crucial Years, 1938–1955* (Clarendon Press, Oxford, 1987).

Tomlinson, J., *Can Governments Manage the Economy?* (Fabian Tract 524, London, 1988).

Tomlinson, J., *Public Policy and the Economy since 1900* (Clarendon Press, Oxford, 1990).

Townsend, Peter, *The Family Life of Old People* (Routledge & Kegan Paul, London, 1957).

Townsend, Peter, *Sociology and Social Policy* (Penguin Press, Harmondsworth, 1976).

Townsend, Peter, *Poverty in the United Kingdom* (Penguin Press, Harmondsworth, 1979).

Townsend, Peter and Bosanquet, Nicholas (eds), *Labour and Inequality* (Fabian Society, London, 1972).

Townsend, Peter and Davidson, N. (eds), *Inequalities in Health: The Black Report* (Penguin Press, London, 1988).

Treble, James H., 'The Attitudes of the Friendly Societies towards the Movement in Great Britain for State Pensions', *International Review of Social History*, 15, 1970, pp. 266–99.

Veit-Wilson, J. H., 'Muddle or Mendacity? The Beveridge Committee and the Poverty Line', *Journal of Social Policy*, 21, 1992, pp. 296–301.

Waley, Sir John, *Social Security – Another British Failure?* (Charles Knight, London, 1972).

Walker, Carol, *Changing Social Policy: The Case of the Supplementary Benefits Review* (Bedford Square Press, London, 1983).

Watkin, Brian, *The National Health Service: The First Phase* (George Allen & Unwin, London, 1978).

Webster, Charles, 'Health, Welfare and Unemployment during the Depression', *Past and Present*, 109, 1985, pp. 204–30.

Webster, Charles, *The Health Services since the War, I: Problems of Health Care: The National Health Service before 1957* (HMSO, London, 1988).

Webster, Charles, 'Conflict and Consensus: Explaining the British Health Service', *20th Century British History*, 1, 2, 1990, pp. 115–51.

Webster, Charles, 'Doctors, Public Service and Profit: General Practitioners and the National Health Service', *Transactions of the Royal Historical Society*, 40, 1990, pp. 197–216.

Weindling, P. (ed.), *The Social History of Occupational Health* (Croom Helm, London, 1985).

Whiteley, Paul and Winyard, Stephen, *Pressure for the Poor* (Methuen, London, 1987).

Whiteside, Noel, 'Welfare Insurance and Casual Labour: A Study of Administrative Intervention in Industrial Employment, 1900–1924', *Economic History Review*, XXXII, 4, 1979, pp. 507–22.

Whiteside, Noel, 'Welfare Legislation and Unions during the First World War', *Historical Journal*, 23, 4, 1980, pp. 857–74, and 'A Reply', *Historical Journal*, 25, 2, 1982, pp. 443–6.

Whiteside, Noel, 'Private Agencies for Public Purposes: Some New

Perspectives on Policy-making in Health Insurance between the Wars', *Journal of Social Policy*, 12, 2, 1983, pp. 165–94.

Whiteside, Noel, 'Wages and Welfare: Trade Unions and Industrial Bargaining before the First World War,' *Bulletin of the Society for the Study of Labour History*, 51, 3, 1986, pp. 21–33.

Whiteside, Noel, 'Unemployment and Health, An Historical Perspective', *Journal of Social Policy*, 17, 2, 1988, pp. 177–94.

Whiteside, Noel, *Bad Times: Unemployment in British Social and Political History* (Faber & Faber, London, 1991).

Williams, Karel, *From Pauperism to Poverty* (Routledge & Kegan Paul, London, 1981).

Williams, Karel and Williams, John (eds), *A Beveridge Reader* (Allen & Unwin, London, 1987).

Williams, Philip M., *Hugh Gaitskell* (Oxford University Press, Oxford, 1979).

Wilson, Arnold and Levy, Hermann, *Industrial Insurance: An Historical and Critical Study* (Oxford University Press, London, 1937).

Wilson, Arnold and Levy, Hermann, *Workmen's Compensation* (Oxford University Press, London, 1939).

Wilson, Arnold and Mackay, G. S., *Old Age Pensions: An Historical and Critical Study* (Oxford University Press, London, 1941).

Wilson, Elizabeth, *Women and the Welfare State* Tavistock Publications, London, 1977).

Winch, Donald, *Economics and Policy* (Hodder & Stoughton, London, 1969).

Winter, J. M., *The Great War and the British People* (Macmillan, London, 1985).

Woodroofe, Kathleen, *From Charity to Social Work* (Routledge & Kegan Paul, London, 1962).

Wootton, Barbara, *Social Science and Social Pathology* (Allen & Unwin, London, 1959).

Worswick, G. D. N. (ed.), *The Concept and Measurement of Involuntary Unemployment* (Allen & Unwin, London, 1976).

Wrigley, Chris (ed.), *A History of British Industrial Relations, II* (Harvester, Brighton, 1987).

Wynn, Margaret, *Family Policy* (Michael Joseph, London, 1970).

Young, H., *The Crossman Affair* (Hamish Hamilton, London, 1976).

Younghusband, Eileen, *Social Work and Social Change* (George Allen & Unwin, London, 1964).

Younghusband, Eileen, *Social Work in Britain, 1950–1975* (George Allen & Unwin, London, 1978).

Index